EARTH
BOUND

Introduction

Imagine you are floating in space. You can see the earth far below, but you have never previously visited and have no real idea what it is like. Luckily you have a powerful lens which allows you to zoom in, Google™ Earth style, on anywhere you choose, eavesdropping on moments in time around the globe.

Rough Guide photographers have been doing this for years, travelling the world aiming to capture the essence of places and the people who live there in a single photo. One day we realized that of the literally hundreds of thousands of images we had, some were so outstanding they deserved to be in a book of their own. All of them reminded us what an amazingly rich and diverse place the world is, and, most importantly, why we started travelling in the first place.

All of the pictures in Earthbound represent a particular aspect of the travel experience, whether it's travelling from A to B, collecting souvenirs, visiting unforgettable monuments – or simply hanging out doing nothing. They are all about a specific location so we've included the longitude/latitude coordinates to enable you to find that place online and fantasize about going there. We've also got our best writers involved to tell us more about what we're seeing.

We spent a long time going through our library of images to find the best ones for this book. We hope you have as much fun looking at them as we had choosing them – and that they inspire you in some way to plan your next trip.

Martin Dunford, Rough Guides Publisher

Using this book

Using our latitude/longitude coordinates and QR codes

All the images featured in Earthbound have longitude/latitude coordinates and QR codes (the things that look like weird, square barcodes). To use the longitude/latitude coordinates, simply type them in to Google™ Maps exactly as you see them in the book. This will take you to the precise online location of each image. Scanning the QR codes with your mobile phone, PDA or laptop will give the image's location within Google™ Maps online.*

The QR codes can be read using pretty much any computer device with a reasonable camera and some compatible software. A good website to select and download the right software for your device is:
http://www.mobile-barcodes.com/qr-code-software/
iPhones can download applications such as *2D sense* and *NeoReader* (both available for free) from the App Store via iTunes Store. It's easy to download and install the software. Either download directly to your device, or via a PC/Mac, and then sync up your device and install the software that way. Your device's manufacturer should be able to provide any further technical assistance via their website.

Go to www.roughguides.com/earthbound for more info and links to help you download the software. Not all devices will be able to use QR codes.

(* Your standard data charges will apply - please check with your network provider for details)

Publishing information

This 1st edition published October 2009 by
Rough Guides Ltd, 80 Strand, London WC2R 0RL
14 Local Shopping Centre, Panchsheel Park, New Delhi 110017, India
Distributed by the Penguin Group
Penguin Books Ltd, 80 Strand, London WC2R 0RL
Penguin Group (USA), 375 Hudson Street, NY 10014, USA
Penguin Group (Australia), 250 Camberwell Road, Camberwell, Victoria 3124, Australia
Penguin Books Canada Ltd, 10 Alcorn Avenue, Toronto, Onatario, Canada M4V 1E4
Penguin Group (NZ), 67 Apollo Drive, Mairangi Bay, Auckland 1310, New Zealand
Typeset in Berthold Akzidenz Grotesk and Din to an original design by Scott Stickland.
Printed and bound in China by South China Printing Co. Ltd
© Rough Guides 2009

A catalogue record for this book is available from the British Library.
ISBN: 978-1-84836-194-2
The publishers have done their best to ensure the accuracy and currency of all the information in Earthbound, however, they can accept no responsibility for any loss, injury, or inconvenience sustained by any traveller as a result of information contained in the guide.
1   3   5   7   9   8   6   4   2

Credits

Design and layout: Scott Stickland, Nicola Erdpresser, Diana Jarvis
Picture editing: Nicole Newman, Mark Thomas, Sarah Cummins, Emily Taylor
Editorial: Natasha Foges, Jo Kirby, Alison Roberts, Karen Parker
Production: Rebecca Short

Contents

Activities
6

Belief
28

Everyday life
50

Food and drink
70

Keepsakes
90

People
134

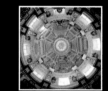
Structures
152

Time–wasting
176

Tourist trail
194

Tradition
220

Activities

Having a great love for the sea, I was excited to see "surfers at Malolo Reef" on my photo-shoot list. I'd made contact with Scobie, a local boat surf-riding legend, who took me out to the reefs. Getting the photo was an amazing balancing act – just when I thought we were about to get wiped out by a wave, Scobie would manoeuvre the boat right at the last moment, allowing me to get the perfect shot.

Chris Christoforou, *Photographer for The Rough Guide to Fiji*

-17.814676, 177.128491
HAWKES PASSAGE, MALOLO BARRIER REEF, FIJI

No dedicated surfer who's serious about the sport can resist Fiji's powerful reef breaks – at their best between April and November. This Pacific paradise hosts a number of international surf competitions, but even casual surfers can benefit from the uncrowded waves along the 30-kilometre length of the Malolo Barrier Reef. World-class waves notwithstanding, a huge part of Fiji's appeal is to be appreciated underwater. Don a mask and snorkel and seek out the deep drop-offs and coral reefs, shimmering colourful fish, sea fans dancing in the current, and manta rays and reef sharks cruising the lagoons. More advanced divers come for the two wrecks: both a World War II B26 bomber and a 40m-long cruise ship, the *Salamander*, blanketed by soft corals and anemones, languish at a depth of nearly 30m.

HUACACHINA, PERU

In the northern reaches of the Atacama – the most arid desert on earth – the lagoon at Huacachina appears like a mirage. An oasis of palm trees and blow-the-budget hotels, it lies hidden among massive sand dunes, some up to 300m high. During the late 1940s, the lagoon became one of Peru's most elegant resorts, and the area continues to draw the crowds, from cure-seekers to sand-surfers – you can rent wooden boards or foot-skis from the cafés along the shoreline. The panorama from the top of the dunes is, of course, stupendous, but for the same views with added adrenaline, hit the sand on a dune-buggy – an exhilarating experience that turns the vast, undulating mounds of sand into a giant roller coaster.

40.412737, -3.749133

PARQUE DE ATRACCIONES, MADRID, SPAIN

In Spain, a rush of blood to the head can often be more fact than figure of speech, at least if you're brave enough to strap yourself into Abismo: the Abyss. Roller coaster seems almost too prosaic a term for this vertebral column of steel, a Dalí-esque construction of coils – the only one of its kind in the world – that pits your stomach (and its contents) against gravity at speeds of up to 100km/hr. As your face turns first white, then scarlet (and maybe even purple), you might just be able to snatch an upside-down, rheumy-eyed view of the rest of Madrid's Parque de Atracciones, over which the Abyss towers to a height of nearly 50m. Sprawling in its shadow are equally hair-raising rides like the 360-degree Tarantula, the Tornado ("wear your shoes well tied", is the official advice) and La Máquina (The Machine), a disconcertingly War of the Worlds-like contraption which promises patrons a loss of "orientation, sense and almost consciousness".

-34.635352, -58.367041

**BUENOS AIRES,
ARGENTINA**

If you've ever wondered why Argentina punches above its weight in international football, a wander through Buenos Aires' poorer barrios should offer a few clues. There is, arguably, no city in the world where the passions of the people are caught up with the sport the way they are here – everywhere you go you'll see people kicking a ball about, and football slogans and platoons of colourful posters are plastered across walls all over town. You'll know when there's a match on: in the days beforehand the entire city talks of nothing else, and while it's being played, life comes to a halt as everyone jostles for space round the nearest TV – everyone who isn't at the stadium, of course. The football obsession of the *hinchadas* (fans) even goes with them to the grave – while the River Plate terraces ring with "yo quiero mi cajón pintado rojo y blanco como mi corazón" ("I want my coffin painted red and white like my heart"), Boca Juniors have taken things a step further and opened a blue-and-yellow-garlanded cemetery for fans.

42.349207, 8.616071

COL DE LA CROIX TO GIROLATA, CORSICA

The three-hour walk from Col de la Croix to Girolata is a popular enough stroll in its own right: the trail hugs the headland, revealing ever more impressive views of the Scandola marine reserve, until you catch your first glimpse of Girolata through the maquis, its Genoese tower and turquoise anchorage set against the red cliffs behind. These days, though, the route is best known for the larger-than-life character of Guy Ceccaldi, the ex-legionnaire who walks it six times a week to deliver the post from nearby Partinello. Since becoming the subject of two often-repeated French television documentaries, white-bearded "Guy le Facteur" has acquired a celebrity status he little dreamt of when he took the job on a dozen or so years ago. Bus parties drive out to applaud his arrival at Col de la Croix on his post-office-issue yellow moped, wearing his trademark 1960s army motorcycle helmet. Having swapped it for a towel to protect him from the heat, Guy poses for photos or heads straight off down the path at zealous speed, depending on his mood.

-22.988300, -43.278601
**SÃO CONRADO,
RIO DE JANEIRO, BRAZIL**

There's no better way of getting your head around the city of Rio in all its variety – from urban sprawl to jungle-clad mountain, teeming beaches to overcrowded favelas – than from 500m up. Tandem hang-gliding flights take off from the southern edge of the Parque Nacional de Tijuca, above the beach at São Conrado. A tentative peek from the ramp reveals treetops far below and the beachfront high-rises of São Conrado in the distance. Then, strapped side by side with your instructor, you charge down the ramp. After the initial surprise of realizing you haven't plummeted to your death, you can start to enjoy yourself, and take in the tranquil views of the mountains, forest and ocean far below. Soaring past a sheer cliff face, feeling the lift as the sea breeze takes you vertically up, is an unforgettable experience. Finally, cruising in over backyard swimming pools, you touch down on the beach, and will probably want to do it all over again – luckily, the experience is preserved on film, meaning you can relive the adrenaline rush for years to come.

10.102997, -84.362469
**LLANO DEL ROSARIO,
COSTA RICA**

There can be few places in the world where you can give
yourself over to gravity in such pristine surroundings as the
Río Colorado in Costa Rica's Valle Central. The languid river
tiptoes around coffee plantations and skirts active volcanoes
as it winds its way north to the Río San Juan and the border
with Nicaragua, cutting through thick jungle buzzing with
toucans and monkeys. At a point just beyond the tiny town
of Llano del Rosario, it ebbs under the rusted steel girders
of the old Río Colorado Bridge – at 70m, one of the highest
bungee bridges in the Americas, and quite clearly picked
for the beauty of the location as much as its extraordinary
height. The essence of bungee jumping has changed
little since the people of Pentecost Island in Vanuatu first
strapped vines to their ankles and hurled themselves off
specially built wooden towers, and it's a simple case of
keeping your nerve through the safety brief, waiting for the
harness and cord to be attached (key consideration, this
one) and then taking the plunge, dropping at dizzying speed
through the forest canopy towards the waters below.

Sport isn't the first thing that comes to mind when you think of Italy. But as well as having a passion for *calcio* (football), Italians are crazy about cycling. The Giro d'Italia, the country's professional cycling race, was first staged in 1909 and is held in May and early June each year. The route of the race is lined with ardent *tifosi* (fans), and the progress of the riders is avidly followed on TV screens across the country. The ultimate prize is the *maglia rosa* (pink jersey), while the *maglia verde* (green jersey) is awarded to the "King of the Mountains", the individual winner of each of the mountain stages. It's a fair accolade – the route includes some punishing climbs, including the painful 1775m of the Grappa massif in the Veneto region. If you fancy some less arduous two-wheeled exploration of rural Italy, there are plenty of specialist operators who will book accommodation and transport your baggage from place to place. You can see the Palladian villas of the Veneto; combine cycling with the country's best grub in Emilia Romagna; take cypress-lined back roads in Tuscany; or discover the rocky and wild landscape of Sardinia.

51.506960, -0.116309

**SOUTHBANK,
LONDON, UK**

The Hayward Gallery, National Theatre, Royal Festival Hall and Queen Elizabeth Hall, with their interconnecting walkways and vast blocks of concrete, are more than just venues. They define a stretch of the river, one now enlivened with art installations and fountains, their brutalist corners home to a happily strolling parade of tourists and locals. For all the scepticism that greeted their 1950s and 1960s construction, you might say that things have turned out just as the council's planners had hoped. Yet the area's architects could not have predicted the cultural intersection that has made the Queen Elizabeth Hall the focus of a street sport developed by Californian surfers. Skateboarders started using the ramps, steps and paved stretches underneath the Hall as a training ground in the early 1970s, while graffiti artists began tagging the walls around them. Needless to say, officialdom was not keen on the development and, while attitudes have softened, the space came close to being redeveloped in 2008. Thankfully the threat has receded, and this can only be a good thing. Set against the chain cafés and high culture of the South Bank, the rattle and thud of skaters – and the improbable acrobatics of the free runners who often congregate nearby – feel like a vital counterpoint, a shot of youthful, vibrant chaos on an otherwise brochure-friendly stretch of riverbank.

-38.014422, 176.345319
KAITUNA RIVER, NEW ZEALAND

Torrents of water cascade from New Zealand's high peaks, and there's enormous fun to be had by hitting the rapids. Rotorua on the North Island has an enviable selection of river runs, which you can tackle aboard rafts, kayaks or, for a more in-your-face experience, by "sledging" – floating down rapids wearing safety gear and clinging to a buoyant plastic sledge. Much of the hype is reserved for the Grade V Kaituna River here, which includes the spectacular Tutea's Falls, a heart-stopping, seven-metre plummet into the churning waters below.

16.563052, 104.745358
SAVANNAKHET, CENTRAL SOUTHERN LAOS

You don't need to be athletic to get your kicks in Laos, but having enough energy to defy gravity is vital if you want to tackle the country's most popular traditional sport. *Kataw* – an ancient, hands-free hotchpotch of volleyball, tennis and football – calls for some serious aerial acrobatics. The main aim is to keep the woven rattan ball off the floor, but chests, heads and legs can all be used, so there's plenty of room for flamboyant mid-air strikes. When *kataw* made its way to Laos from the Sultanate of Malacca more than 500 years ago, it was mostly played by men and boys standing in circles. Since then, 1.5-metre-high nets have been introduced and the competitive game has gone on to become something of a national obsession: matches take place right around the country – everywhere from the dusty banks of the Mekong River to inner-city schoolyards. When you see one in action, return the players' welcoming smiles and it'll only be a matter of time before you're invited to step up to the net. Just don't attempt a bicycle kick on your first go.

34.018984, -116.163790
JOSHUA TREE NATIONAL PARK, CALIFORNIA, USA

Joshua Tree National Park bridges the divide between the Colorado and Mojave deserts in a vast, silent area of craggy trees. Almost 800,000 acres have been set aside for the park's gnarled namesakes, which flourish in an otherwise sparsely vegetated landscape, forming a perfect counterpoint to surreal clusters of monzogranite boulders, great rock piles pushed up from the earth by the movements of the Pinto Mountain Fault running directly below. Often as tall as 30m, their edges are rounded and smooth from thousands of years of flash floods and winds, but there are enough nodules, fissures and irregularities to make this superb rock-climbing territory.

29.626056, 35.432281

WADI RUM, JORDAN

You shouldn't leave Jordan without having visited the incredible desert moonscape of Wadi Rum – once the haunt of Lawrence of Arabia – south of the Shara mountains. This rocky landscape, rising up to 800m sheer from the desert floor, has been weathered over millennia into bulbous domes and weird ridges and textures that look like nothing so much as molten candle-wax, but it's the sheer bulk of these mountains that awes – some with vertical, smooth flanks, others scarred and distorted, seemingly dripping and melting under the burning sun. The intervening corridors of soft red sand only add to the image of the mountains as monumental islands in a dry sea; split through by networks of canyons and ravines, they offer opportunities galore for scrambling and rock climbing, as well as camel and horse trekking – you could ride for hours or days without seeing another soul.

-33.905226, 151.269328

BRONTE SWIMMING BATHS, SYDNEY

High surf days are the best. Effortless strokes pull you along the smooth surface of the turquoise water, and as your head rolls up for air you catch sight of a huge plume of white spray as another Pacific roller crashes against the concrete sea wall. It's a scene replayed all along Sydney's shoreline, where just about every beach has its pool. The one at Bronte – wedged between sea, beach and suburbia-topped rocky headland – is one of the most venerable, dating from 1887 when sea bathing was in its neck-to-toe-woollen-swimsuit infancy. It is free to enter and can be a wonderfully egalitarian and cosmopolitan place. City bankers rub muscled shoulders with shop assistants before work, and as the morning wears on they're replaced by mothers with young kids, students and backpackers. The bodies may be bronzed but it's not about being beautiful. The beaches are for the poseurs – here, it's all about the swimming. Even in the chilly depths of winter you'll see crack-of-dawn stalwarts padding across the weathered concrete and diving in without hesitation, but the ideal time is late on a languid summer's afternoon – don't forget to bring a sundowner.

-22.970659, -43.182836
**RIO DE JANEIRO,
BRAZIL**

Maintaining an even tan and impressive musculature is still the principal occupation of most of Rio's beachgoers, who break up periods of swimming, posing and cerveja-drinking with bouts of body-sculpting activity. Joggers, cyclists and skateboarders swarm up and down the pavements, musclemen sweat it out at the parallel bars at Arpoador and Flamengo, and beach football on Copacabana beach is as strong a tradition as legend would have it – there's no problem getting a game, though playing on loose sand amidst highly skilled practitioners of Brazil's national sport certainly has the potential for humiliation.

25.216139, 55.291872
**NAD AL SHEBA,
DUBAI**

The district of Nad Al Sheba – most of it still untouched desert – is home to one of Dubai's quirkier attractions: the Camel Racecourse. Races are held here from about 7am during the winter months, but even if no events are scheduled, you can come and watch the animals being exercised early in the morning. It's a captivating sight: literally hundreds of colourfully dressed beasts and their heavily robed riders amble – and occasionally gallop – across the desert, while their owners charge after them in 4WDs shrieking encouragement.

-38.081553, 176.187884

**ROTORUA,
NEW ZEALAND**

Just about every bus touring New Zealand's North Island stops at the Agrodome, where the star attractions are a 45-minute sheep show, featuring sheep-shearing, lamb-feeding and the like, and the adjacent Agrodome Adventure Park, where adrenaline junkies get their fix. Attractions include a 43-metre bungee jump, the Agrojet, where tiny racing jetboats hurtle around a short course, and the Freefall Extreme, which simulates freefalling using a powerful propeller and safety net above which you hover – or at least try to – five metres up. If that doesn't seem like enough fun, try the Zorb, another Kiwi-pioneered adrenaline rush, which involves diving into the centre of a huge clear plastic ball and rolling down a two-hundred-metre hill – or taking the slower but wilder zigzag course. You can choose from wet and dry rides – the former option, inevitably, being the more fun.

58.637793, -155.492249

KATMAI NATIONAL PARK, ALASKA, USA

The small bush community of King Salmon, Alaska, scattered alongside the broad Naknek River, was once a Cold War military base. Such is its remoteness, there's no reason to come here – except, perhaps, for some solitary fishing. 22km downstream, the Bristol Bay fishing village of Naknek is the scene of the world's largest sockeye run, with some twenty million fish passing between mid-June and the end of July. Around seventy percent of the world's red salmon is caught in Bristol Bay and three-quarters of those are fished out of the river in and around Naknek. Once the season opens, fishing boats are gunwhale to gunwhale vying to be first to get their nets in the water, and sleepy King Salmon and Naknek are overrun with visiting fishermen.

51.582425, -4.291191

**GOWER PENINSULA,
WALES, UK**

A 25-kilometre peninsula of undulating limestone, Gower
is a world of its own, pointing down into the Bristol Channel
to the west of Swansea. The area is fringed by sweeping
yellow bays and precipitous cliffs, caves and blowholes to the
south, and wide, flat marshes and cockle beds to the north,
with brackened heath and tiny villages in between. Gower's
western edge – a wild, frilly series of inlets and cliffs – is
dominated by the spectacular Rhossili Bay. A six-kilometre
yawn of white sand stretching into the distance, the beach
offers some of Wales' best opportunities for surfing, and
paragliders flock here for the aerial views of Worm's Head, at
Gower's westernmost point: an isolated string of rocks with
the spectacular appearance of a Welsh dragon at low tide.

9.494897, 76.317472

**KERALA,
INDIA**

Practised in special earth-floored gyms and pits across the state, *kalarippayattu* is Kerala's unique martial art – a distinctive brand of acrobatic combat drawing heavily on yoga and ancient Indian knowledge of the human body. Although formalized in the twelfth century by the bodyguards of medieval warlords and chieftains, its origins are believed to stretch back two thousand years or more. Once initiated, students are taught a complex set of strenuous exercises designed to render their bodies strong and flexible: kicks, jumps, animal postures, spins, step sequences and vigorous stretches, joined in increasingly complicated sequences. Once they've mastered the set moves, students are eventually introduced to combat with various terrifying weapons, including swords and spears. The final stage, *verum kaythari*, focuses on barehanded combat against an armed enemy – and is for advanced practitioners only.

44.800127, 1.620183
**ROCAMADOUR,
FRANCE**

Renting a canoe for a gentle paddle down the Dordogne and Vézère rivers – or cycling and horseriding along the tree-lined riverbanks – are popular activities for outdoorsy types, but take a ride in a hot-air balloon and you'll be treated to panoramic views of one of France's most stunning regions. Trips typically last an hour and depart in the early morning or late afternoon when the winds have died down, soaring silently over sprawling meadows, oak forest valleys, majestic chateaux and honey-stone villages. If the conditions are favourable, don't miss the opportunity to float by the spectacular cliff-top village of Rocamadour – a pilgrimage site since the Middle Ages, as it harbours the tomb of Zaccheus of Jericho, a Christian hermit. As you survey the stone houses, churches and medieval fortress, chiselled into the limestone cliffs, spare a thought for the poor pilgrims, many of whom climb the 216 steps to the top of the rocky plateau on their knees.

Belief

The moment I stepped through the gate of Istanbul's Blue Mosque and walked across the enormous courtyard, I was in awe of the imposing structure, with its massive dome and multiple minarets. But it was the mosque's interior that really stopped me in my tracks: a vast space, it's decorated with intricate Iznik tiles and filled with a calm serenity.

Roger d'Olivere Mapp, *Photographer for The Rough Guide to Istanbul*

41.005303, 28.976907
BLUE MOSQUE, ISTANBUL, TURKEY

With its six slender minarets and cascade of domes, the Blue Mosque is one of Istanbul's most striking monuments. Before construction began in 1609, objections were raised to the plan of a six-minareted mosque: it was said to be unholy to rival the six minarets of the mosque at Mecca, and – perhaps more pertinently – it would be a drain on state revenues. The true cause of the objections, however, probably had more to do with the need to bulldoze several palaces belonging to imperial ministers to make way for construction. Inside, four "elephant foot" pillars – so called because of their gargantuan size, some five metres across – impose their disproportionate dimensions on the interior, appearing squashed against the outer walls. But it's the predominantly blue colour of the ceiling, covered in some twenty thousand mosaic tiles, that leaves the most enduring impression – such a glorious sight that gazing up at them is worth the neck-ache.

-53.152965, -70.897125

PUNTA ARENAS, PATAGONIA, CHILE

The first thing that strikes you about the magnificent cemetery at Punta Arenas is its vastness – it covers four city blocks – but further exploration reveals a fascinating reflection of Patagonia's turbulent history in marble and stone. Crisscrossed by a network of footpaths lined with immaculately clipped cypresses, the cemetery is an intriguing place to wander around. The simple statue of a solitary Fuegian Indian is dwarfed by the ostentatious mausoleums constructed at the end of the last century, while the solemn epitaphs on the headstones of the pioneers and sailors from Britain, Spain, Croatia and Italy, interred far from their native soil, make for an intriguingly eclectic necropolis.

33.253906, -115.472628

**SALVATION MOUNTAIN,
CALIFORNIA, USA**

The one sight you really shouldn't miss around southern California's Salton Sea is Salvation Mountain – a fantastic work of large-scale religious folk art that has been worked at continuously since 1985 by its founder, friendly local eccentric Leonard Knight. He has devoted his later life to this wildly coloured mass of straw and adobe, liberally painted with extracts from the Bible and exhortations to "Repent" – there's even an abandoned motorboat to represent Noah's Ark. Leonard adds to his structure – already 9m high and 30m wide – each morning, but spends much of the day guiding the trickle of visitors; a small donation is appreciated but never requested.

30.317827, 30.354452
**WADI NATRUN,
EGYPT**

The quasi-oasis of Wadi Natrun, just off the Desert Road between Cairo and Alexandria, is famous for its four walled monasteries, which date back to the dawn of Christian monasticism, providing spiritual leadership for Egypt's Copts for the last 1500 years. The monastic day begins at 3am with an hour of silent prayer in individual cells, before two hours of collective worship in the chapel, followed by unrelenting labour until the main meal of the day at noon. Afterwards, the monks work until 5pm, assemble for prayers and then return to their tasks until sheer exhaustion forces them to bed. Black garments symbolize their death to the world of bodily desires; their hoods are embroidered with twelve crosses, after Christ's disciples.

**SAVANNAKHET,
LAOS**

Most ethnic Lao men become novice monks at some time
in their lives, usually before marriage. Monks take vows to
uphold no less than 227 precepts, ranging from abstinence
from sexual relations, alcohol and the wearing of any sort of
ornamentation to more arcane rules such as a prohibition on
urinating while standing upright (so as not to soil their robes).
A man who has yet to do time in a monastery is referred to
as *dip* or "unripe", alluding to the fact that many Lao don't
consider a man complete without some time spent in the
monastery; before the advent of public schools, lessons in
reading and writing at the monastery were about all the
education the average Lao could hope for.

59.940112, 30.328799

CHURCH OF THE SAVIOUR ON SPILLED BLOOD, ST PETERSBURG, RUSSIA

The Church of the Saviour on Spilled Blood is one of St Petersburg's most striking landmarks, standing out against the predominantly Baroque and Neoclassical architecture of the rest of the city. The spilled blood was that of Tsar Alexander II, who was assassinated on this spot on March 1, 1881, by the Nihilist terrorist group known as the People's Will. In the event, the first bomb thrown at the Tsar missed, but instead of fleeing the scene, Alexander chose to berate his would-be assassin, who was himself injured. A second assassin lobbed another bomb, which this time hit its target. Although work began on the church almost immediately, it wasn't finished until 1907. During the 1930s, the Communists briefly turned the church into a museum celebrating the assassination, until Stalin thought his subjects might get some useful tips, after which it was used as a warehouse. Now fully restored, the church is well worth a visit: its interior is decorated from floor to ceiling with over 7500 square metres of mosaics – more than any other church in the world.

28.419524, -81.581190

CINDERELLA CASTLE, DISNEY WORLD, FLORIDA, USA

Whatever your attitude toward theme parks, there's no denying that Disney World is the pacesetter, delivering escapism at its most technologically advanced and psychologically brilliant in a multitude of ingenious guises. In a crime-free environment where wholesome, all-American values hold sway, Disney World often makes the real world – and all its problems – seem like a distant memory. The whimsical Cinderella Castle, smack in the middle of Disney's Magic Kingdom, makes a fitting centrepiece for a place that emphasizes escapism and family fun over thrills and spills. A stunning 57-metre pseudo-Rhineland palace, the castle looks as though it should be the most elaborate ride in the park; in fact, it's merely a shell that conceals all the electronics that drive the whole extravaganza. Of all the efforts to create an aura of fantasy, though, the nightly Wishes fireworks display manages to strike the most magical note, casting a spell over the assembled crowds – and daily attendance figures of 100,000 visitors show that the popularity of this rose-tinted wonderland shows no signs of abating.

-22.974138, -43.225139
**JOCKEY CLUB,
RIO DE JANEIRO, BRAZIL**

In the shadow of Rio's world-famous Christ statue and at the shore of a tranquil inland lake, there can't be many racecourses in the world that enjoy as dramatic a location as the Jockey Club. With its imposing Louis XV-style facade, the club has been a byword for tradition and sophistication since its inauguration in the 1920s, but nowadays, all comers are welcome. Business executives and politicians take their place in the high stands, complete with waiter service and table-top telephones to place their bets, while down below on wooden benches, the animated banter of workers old and young breaks into raucous shouting, cursing and paper-waving as the horses thunder round the course. For some, a fortune is at stake, but for most, it's a matter of a few reais and a bit of pride amongst friends. If you fancy a flutter, head for the betting parlours, where savvy punters will be more than happy to share their tips.

38.111787, 13.339376
**CONVENTO DEI CAPPUCCINI,
PALERMO, ITALY**

For several hundred years, Palermo's Capuchin monks retained their own burial ground, placing their dead in catacombs under the church attached to their monastery. Later, following bequests from rich laymen, others began to be interred here, right up until 1881; all in all, some eight thousand bodies were preserved by various chemical and drying processes – including dehydration, the use of vinegar and arsenic baths, and treatment with quicklime. The rough-cut stone corridors are divided according to sex and status, with different caverns reserved for men, women, the clergy, doctors, lawyers and surgeons. Suspended in individual niches and pinned with an identifying tag, the bodies are vile, contorted, grinning figures, some decomposed beyond recognition, others complete with skin, hair and eyes, fixing you with a steely stare. Those that aren't arranged along the walls lie in stacked glass coffins; it is, to say the least, an unnerving experience to walk among them.

11.303821, 106.133181
CAO DAI CATHEDRAL, TAY NINH, VIETNAM

Ngo Van Chieu, a Vietnamese civil servant and spiritualist, was first contacted by a superior spirit calling itself Cao Dai, or "high place", in the early 1920s. Instructed to adopt the Divine Eye as a representation of the spirit's existence, Ngo set about evangelizing, and Cao Dai – a fusion of eastern and western religions – had attracted 500,000 followers by 1930. Today, the religion continues to thrive in its twin power bases of Tay Ninh District and the Mekong Delta. The religion's eclectic ideology is mirrored in the interior of the Cao Dai Great Temple, which a dazzled Graham Greene described as a "Walt Disney fantasia of the East": part cathedral and part pagoda, it draws together a clutter of icons and elements under a vaulted ceiling, and daubs them all with the Day-Glo hues of a Hindu temple.

9.288102, 79.317604
RAMESHWARAM TEMPLE, TAMIL NADU, INDIA

Hindus tend to be followers of either Vishnu or Shiva, but the sacred island of Rameshwaram, at Tamil Nadu's southeastern tip, brings the two together, as this is where the god Rama, an incarnation of Vishnu, worshipped Shiva in the Ramayana. One of South India's holiest pilgrimage sites, the temple here is distinctive for its corridors, their extreme length – 205m, flanked by 1212 massive pillars – giving a remarkable impression of receding perspective. Before entering the inner sections, pilgrims are expected to bathe at each of the 22 *tirthas* (tanks) in the temple – hence the groups of dripping-wet pilgrims, most of them fully clothed, making their way from one tank to the next to be doused in a bucket of water by a temple attendant. Each *tirtha* is said to have special benefits: one provides relief from debt, another gives "complete wisdom", and a third promises long life for women, as well as "the love of their spouses".

7.855434, 80.651300
GOLDEN TEMPLE, DAMBULLA, SRI LANKA

No two Sri Lankan temples are exactly alike. Some occupy a few caves buried in thick jungle; others comprise the remains of great monastic foundations that originally supported thousands of monks. The dusty little town of Dambulla is a case in point. It's most famous for its magical, dimly lit cave temples, which harbour little masterpieces of Sinhalese Buddhist art and seem to glow with the rich reds and golds of the statues and paintings that fill them. At the bottom of the steps up to the cave temples, the bizarre Golden Temple – a shamelessly kitsch building topped by a thirty-metre-high golden Buddha – stops you in your tracks. As though reacting to the money-grubbing circus of the modern-day temple, the normally beatific Buddha looks a little less than serene.

-22.912167, -43.230164
MARACANÃ STADIUM, RIO DE JANEIRO, BRAZIL

Rio's Maracanã Stadium is the biggest of its kind in the world. Built in two years by ten thousand labourers in time for the 1950 World Cup, it now holds over 100,000 people – though at the final match of the 1950 tournament 199,854 spectators crammed in to watch Brazil lose to Uruguay in what was deemed a national catastrophe. Conceived first and foremost as a monument to demonstrate Brazil's arrival as a nation to the rest of the world, the Maracanã today stands as the country's major statement of footballing prowess; and Brazil's successful bid for the 2014 World Cup – the final of which will be held here – is set to propel the country's passion for the sport to fervid new heights. The stadium is the home ground of local clubs Flamengo and Fluminense, and well over 100,000 fans – bedecked in their team's colours and sporting all manner of colourful accessories – pack the ground for the lively "Fla-Flu" derbies. Attending a game here is one of the most extraordinary experiences Rio has to offer, even if you don't like football – the theatrical spectacle and the palpable devotion of the fans alone make it worth the trip.

11.884518, 75.368652

**KERALA,
INDIA**

The Keralan ritual dances known as *theyyam* are held for all kinds of reasons: to celebrate the safe return of a son from the Gulf, the construction of a new house or as part of a temple feast. And they come in an amazing number of different shapes and sizes, each with its own distinctive make-up, costume and outlandish masks – some *theyyam* performers don huge headdresses made of crimson-painted papier-mâché, metal studwork and tassles, framing meticulously painted faces and bodies loaded with jewellery and heavy costumes. The bodies of performers are believed to be literally possessed by the deities themselves; as the god or goddess moves among the crowd, its spirit glares through the performer's bloodshot eyes, animating his every move and gesture. It's hard to convey the electric mix of terror and adoration such visions invoke among onlookers.

31.776767, 35.234077

**WAILING WALL, JERUSALEM,
ISRAEL**

Set high up in the Judaean hills and founded 3,000 years ago by King David, Jerusalem holds some of the world's most sacred structures, aglow with millennia of reverence, devotion and inspiration. The heart of this holiest of places is the Old City, whose four quarters – Jewish, Armenian, Christian and Muslim – are testament to its importance in the world's three great monotheistic religions. As the quintessential ancient-meets-modern settlement, anachronism is everywhere you look. It's catching glimpses of this juxtaposition of non sequiturs – garbed zealots lingering on mobile calls or young Israeli hipsters bowing their heads in prayer – that make visiting a BC town in the twenty-first century AD such a meaningful experience.

14.565649, -89.351807
**ESQUIPULAS,
GUATEMALA**

All year round, a steady stream of buses wind through the hills of eastern Guatemala, beneath craggy outcrops and forested peaks, to reach the town of Esquipulas: site of the most important Catholic shrine in Central America. The pilgrims come for a glimpse of a sixteenth-century statue of Christ, carved from a dark wood to appeal to the local people, and credited with miraculous healing powers. On the principal day of pilgrimage, January 15, the town is full to bursting, as buses chartered from all over Guatemala choke the streets, while the most devoted pilgrims arrive on foot, some dropping to their knees for the last few kilometres. Inside, there's a scurry of hushed devotion amid clouds of smoke and incense. Pilgrims approach the image on their knees, while others light candles, mouth supplications or simply stand in silent crowds. Back outside, the streets swarm with souvenir and relic hawkers, and pilgrims who, duty done, head off to eat and drink away the rest of their stay.

33.607923, -7.632816
**MOSQUÉE HASSAN II,
CASABLANCA, MOROCCO**

For many years lacking in sights, Casablanca's fortunes changed when on July 9, 1980, King Hassan II declared his wish for the city to be endowed with "a large, fine building of which it can be proud until the end of time". Work on the Mosquée Hassan II – a vast complex raised on a rocky platform reclaimed from the ocean – was duly launched the same year and the building inaugurated on August 30, 1993. Looking towards it from the city centre, its huge size tricks you into thinking it's far nearer – and smaller – than it really is. In fact, its minaret is two hundred metres high, making it the tallest in the world – a laser on its summit projects a beam towards Mecca – while the mosque itself provides space for 25,000 worshippers inside, and a further 80,000 in its courtyard. As a building, it's second only to Mecca's in size, and St Peter's in Rome could fit comfortably inside. Unusually, it's open to all, on accompanied one-hour visits.

31.949737, 35.934622
KING HUSSEIN MOSQUE, AMMAN, JORDAN

Observant Muslims pray five times a day, the exact times being set in advance by the religious authorities. The faithful are called to prayer by the muezzin; in previous centuries, he would climb the minaret of the mosque and summon by shouting, but almost everywhere in Jordan this tradition has now been overtaken either by a taped call to prayer or by amplification. Nonetheless, the sound has a captivating beauty all its own, especially down in the echoing valleys of Amman when dozens of mosques are calling simultaneously, repeating in long, melodious strings: "God is most great! (Allahu akbar!) I testify that there is no god but God. I testify that Muhammad is the Messenger of God. Come to prayer, come to salvation. God is most great!" The dawn call has an extra phrase added: "Prayer is better than sleep."

37.731645, 128.592782
**WOLJEONGSA TEMPLE,
GANGWON-DO, SOUTH KOREA**

Never-ending rows of colour-free cars and identical apartment blocks may lead visitors to believe that Korea's obsession with conformity is a modern invention. However, head to one of the country's ubiquitous temples and you'll see that its source – an overlay of Confucian and Buddhist ideals – not only goes back quite a while, but is a great deal easier to digest. Beyond the neat rows of shoes by the entrance are little islands of tranquillity where you'll find groups of droning monks, clutches of *kimchi* pots and lines of calligraphic poetry, all surrounded by wooden buildings with eaves and innards meticulously painted in the five colours of local Buddhism. In a country where neon and noise are now the order of the day, it may take a little while to adjust to the more subtle tugs on the senses. But linger awhile to take in the temple's contours and colours – evidence of an artistic balance that was once the envy of East Asia – then close your eyes and breathe in, and the wafts of pine and incense, the trickling streams and the rhythmic clack of wood will soon make the outside world seem a very distant place.

10.481448, -61.474643

WATERLOO, TRINIDAD

The gleaming white, onion-domed Waterloo Temple is an odd sight, surrounded at high tide by fishing boats and by extensive mud flats at low. With its funeral pyres at the water's edge and multicoloured prayer flags flapping in the breeze, you could be forgiven for thinking you were standing on the banks of the River Ganges. But this octagonal temple has served the Hindu community of central Trinidad since the mid-twentieth century, when it was founded by Sewdass Sadhu, an Indian labourer. Using a bicycle to ferry the foundation rocks into the water and placing barrels full of concrete on the sea floor at low tide, Sewdass painstakingly built up the temple single-handed – a Sisyphean task which took 25 years to complete.

27.710014, 85.348830

KATHMANDU, NEPAL

With trident-shaped *tikas* painted on their foreheads, hair knotted into dreadlocks, exposed, ash-covered bodies and mysterious amulets, *sadhus* are an evocative presence at Hindu temples in Kathmandu and throughout Nepal. These solitary, wandering holy men have renounced worldly possessions and devoted their lives to achieving spiritual liberation. Although there are many types, most *sadhus* in Nepal are Shaivas – followers of Shiva, many of whose romantic and ascetic adventures took place in the country's valleys and mountains. There is no single route to enlightenment for these pilgrims: yoga, meditation, quiet contemplation and consumption of drugs such as ganja (cannabis) are all common. Some unorthodox *sadhus*, however, opt for more extreme behaviour: in an attempt to escape the fear of death, Aghori ascetics live on cremation grounds, consume unpleasant food from cranial bowls, indulge in sexual activities with lower caste and menstruating women, and even – so it is said – take part in cannibalism.

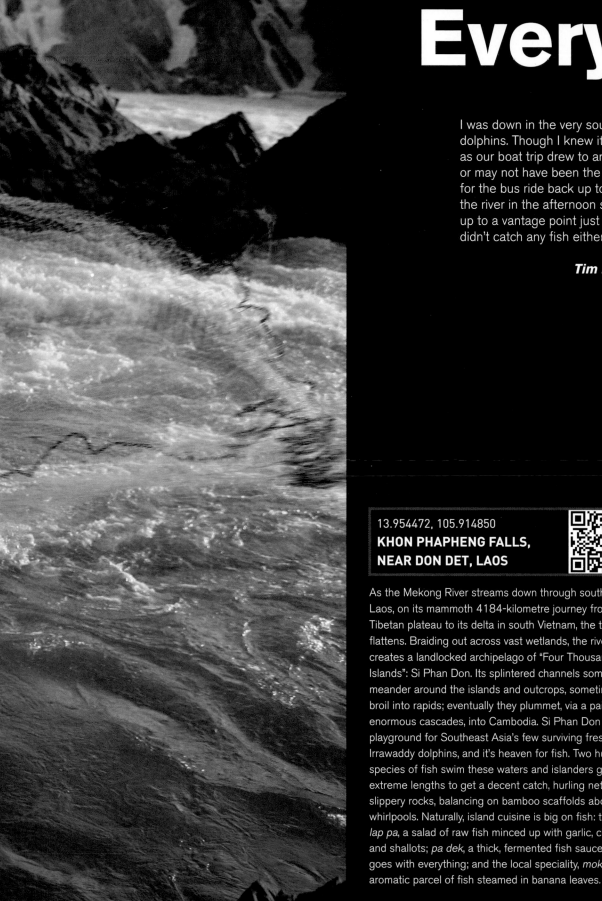

Everyday life

I was down in the very southern tip of Laos, trying to photograph the Irrawaddy dolphins. Though I knew it was an almost impossible task, I still felt disappointed as our boat trip drew to an end – a few splashes and flashes of grey that may or may not have been the elusive dolphins, but no pictures. I was getting ready for the bus ride back up to the islands when I saw a man casting his net across the river in the afternoon sunlight. I quickly scrambled across rocks and climbed up to a vantage point just in time to get this picture. Despite his efforts, he didn't catch any fish either.

Tim Draper, Photographer for The Rough Guide to Laos

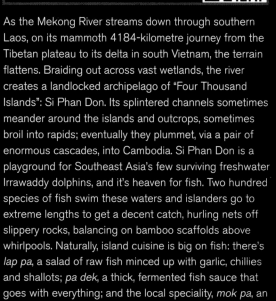

13.954472, 105.914850
**KHON PHAPHENG FALLS,
NEAR DON DET, LAOS**

As the Mekong River streams down through southern Laos, on its mammoth 4184-kilometre journey from the Tibetan plateau to its delta in south Vietnam, the terrain flattens. Braiding out across vast wetlands, the river creates a landlocked archipelago of "Four Thousand Islands": Si Phan Don. Its splintered channels sometimes meander around the islands and outcrops, sometimes broil into rapids; eventually they plummet, via a pair of enormous cascades, into Cambodia. Si Phan Don is a playground for Southeast Asia's few surviving freshwater Irrawaddy dolphins, and it's heaven for fish. Two hundred species of fish swim these waters and islanders go to extreme lengths to get a decent catch, hurling nets off slippery rocks, balancing on bamboo scaffolds above whirlpools. Naturally, island cuisine is big on fish: there's *lap pa*, a salad of raw fish minced up with garlic, chillies and shallots; *pa dek*, a thick, fermented fish sauce that goes with everything; and the local speciality, *mok pa*, an aromatic parcel of fish steamed in banana leaves.

55.977265, -3.170052
CUSTOMS WHARF, LEITH, SCOTLAND

Although Leith is generally known as the port of Edinburgh, it developed independently of the city up the hill, its history bound up in the hard graft of fishing, shipbuilding and trade. An intriguing place to explore, it's worth visiting not just for the contrasts to central Edinburgh, but also for its nautical air, excellent seafood and well-worn, friendly pubs. Leith's initial revival from down-and-out port to des-res waterfront, which began in the 1980s, is now gathering pace. Alongside the stately royal yacht *Britannia*, now settled into her retirement, the massive docks are being transformed at a rate of knots.

40.851173,14.257896

CENTRO STORICO, NAPLES, ITALY

As a city that's always been more famous for its mafiosi than its monuments, Naples comes with plenty of baggage. And first impressions can often make you want to get on the first train out: grimy, sprawling and chaotic, it's light years away from daintily packaged Venice, sophisticated Florence or suave Milan. But scratch the surface and you'll discover that Naples has its own unique brand of charm. Rather than pandering to its visitors, this city keeps it real: refreshingly lacking in tourist-ready gloss, Naples is beautiful, but unassumingly so. Down-at-heel churches are crammed with Baroque masterpieces; rustic trattorie serve up world-class cuisine; and a simple stroll through the crowded, buzzing streets of the historic centre yields no end of photo opportunities. It may have been overlooked for years, but now more and more visitors are falling for Naples' irresistible, rough-and-ready charm; this is Italy at its unpredictable, high-octane best.

51.514235, -0.152419
**SELFRIDGE'S,
LONDON, UK**

A huge Edwardian pile fronted by giant Ionic columns, Selfridge's lords it over Oxford Street, London's busiest
shopping thoroughfare. The store was opened in 1909 by Chicago millionaire Gordon Selfridge, who flaunted its
130 departments with the slogan, "Why not spend a day at Selfridge's?". The shop is credited with selling the world's
first television set, as well as introducing the concept of the "bargain basement", "the customer is always right", the
stress-inducing "only ten more shopping days to Christmas" countdown, and the heady bouquet of perfumes from the
cosmetics counters, strategically placed at the entrance to all department stores to entice customers in. A century after
its opening, the shop has managed to establish itself as a bastion of luxury and taste. Whether it involves selling Parisian
macaroons in the foodhall or buffing the Gucci bags to a mirror-like sheen in the Accessories department, a job here is
a touch more glamorous than your average stint on the shop floor.

23.133608, -82.361063

HAVANA,
CUBA

Though more famous for its son, salsa and Chevrolets, don't be surprised if you catch a whiff of greasepaint along with the cigar smoke in downtown Havana, and not only during Carnaval. While the endemically effusive nature of the native Habaneros lends a sense of the theatrical to even the most mundane of daily routines, there are plenty of Cubans who actually make their living from the stage, be it street, screen or circus ring. The late clown Trompoloco – alias actor/comedian Edwin Fernández – was one of the best loved, and Havana's premier big top is named in his honour. This is where performers from all over Latin America converge each summer for the annual Circuba festival, a fortnight-long circus extravaganza featuring *payasos* (clowns) of every stripe and gravity-defying tightrope walkers who seem to test out Che Guevara's mantra: ¡Patria o Muerte! Many of them are graduates of Havana's highly respected National Circus School, and some have scooped top prizes abroad. This being Cuba, of course, clowning around has become a revolution in itself, and you don't necessarily need a ticket to see it. Gigantería, Havana's most visible street theatre troupe, have been sending their tottering, conga-banging stilt-walkers around the city's old town since the turn of the millennium, parading away everyday hardships just as all Cubans continue to laugh in the face of adversity.

43.770588, 11.247460

SAN FREDIANO, FLORENCE, ITALY

Think of a great city, and the chances are that there's a river running through it: New York, Paris, Rome, London, Tokyo, Cairo – rivers were crucial to the development of all of them. Florence is no different: founded by the Romans on the banks of the Arno, it rapidly grew to become a powerful trading centre, and its financiers became the richest on the continent. Just as Paris has its Left and Right banks, so Florence's north and south sides are quite distinct. The former – known to the locals as *Arno di quà* ("over here") – is home to most of Florence's world-famous sights, while the south side – *Arno di là* ("over there") or, more formally, the Oltrarno ("beyond the Arno") – belongs far more to the Florentines than to the visitors. Wandering the tranquil streets surrounding the church of San Frediano, it's easy to forget that you're in a city so heavily reliant on tourism.

34.066104, -4.970959

CHOUWARA, FES, MOROCCO

There is a compulsive fascination about the tanneries at Chouwara. Cascades of water pour through holes that were once the windows of houses, hundreds of skins lie spread out on the rooftops to dry, while amid the vats of dye and pigeon dung (used to treat the leather), tanners treat the skins. The rotation of colours in the honeycombed vats follows a traditional sequence – yellow (supposedly "saffron", in fact turmeric), red (poppy), blue (indigo), green (mint) and black (antimony) – although vegetable dyes have largely been replaced by chemicals, to the detriment of workers' health. This innovation and the occasional rinsing machine aside, there has been little change here since the sixteenth century, when Fes replaced Córdoba as the pre-eminent city of leather production. As befits such an ancient system, the ownership is also intricately feudal: the foremen run a hereditary guild and the workers pass down their specific jobs from generation to generation.

26.919000, 70.892018
**RAJASTHAN,
INDIA**

A snapshot of Rajasthan at its most iconic: the man, with his colourful orange turban, golden earring and imposing moustache, and his camel, looking perhaps even more aloof, as they stop for a break amidst the scrubby sands of the Thar desert. In the arid wastes of Rajasthan, the hardy and self-sufficient camel is undoubtedly king, used since time immemorial to transport people and produce from town to town, and the sight of these aristocratic animals remains one of India's most evocative images, whether seen navigating the desert sands towards dusk, or mincing haughtily through the chaotic rush-hour traffic of one of the state's bustling cities. The camel's crucial role in local life is celebrated at the world-famous Pushkar Camel Fair, held annually in November, when Rajasthanis from across the state converge on the small town of Pushkar, with as many as forty thousand camels in tow, to trade animals and swap gossip. More recently, the state's dromedaries have experienced a new and vital lease of life ferrying tourists out into the deserts around Bikaner, Jodhpur and, especially, Jaisalmer, on romantic "camel safaris" – one of the must-do items on the lists of most visitors to India's incomparable desert state.

-33.877989, 151.242766

DOUBLE BAY, SYDNEY, AUSTRALIA

You'll need to dress up if you're to fit in when sipping a skinny latte in the cafés of Double Bay. For this is Sydney's wealthiest suburb – the southern hemisphere's answer to Rodeo Drive. Swimming-pooled mansions and boutique hotels pepper the hills, from where the tree-lined boulevards slope down to Sydney Harbour, where sleek yachts languidly await their owners. Set a little back from the water, the lanes running off Knox Street exude the five-star glitz that has become synonymous with the place – "DB" to residents and regulars, "Double Pay" to those who can only dream. Glammed-up socialites teeter between chichi boutiques where top Australian labels such as Carla Zampatti and Collette Dinnigan rub haute couture shoulders with Diane von Furstenberg and Givenchy. But it's not just about the clothes. The exacting demands of Double Bay's groomed and manicured residents are met by elegant nail bars, pricey shoe shops and the sort of hair salon whose customers are coiffed to glossy perfection as they perch on Philippe Starck chairs.

40.419485, -3.692265
PLAZA DE CIBELES, MADRID, SPAIN

Whatever Barcelona or San Sebastián might claim, the Madrid scene, immortalized in the movies of Pedro Almodóvar, is still the most vibrant in Spain. As you get to grips with the city, you soon realize that it's the lifestyle of its inhabitants – the *madrileños* – that makes the capital such a fun place to be. They enjoy an enviably fun-packed existence, whether hanging out in traditional cafés, packing the lanes of the Sunday flea market or playing hard and very late in a thousand bars, clubs, discos and *tascas*. The nightlife, in particular, is a pretty serious phenomenon: the *madrileños* are nicknamed *los gatos* or "the cats" for their nocturnal lifestyle, and this is one of the few cities in Europe whose roads can be gridlocked in the early hours of the morning, when locals are either heading home or moving on to the dance-past-dawn clubs.

-6.237994, 39.535546
BWEJUU, ZANZIBAR, TANZANIA

One of Zanzibar's biggest earners these days is seaweed, or *mwani*, of which over ten thousand tons are exported annually to the Far East. Seaweed cultivation was introduced to southeastern Unguja two decades ago as an income-generating project for local women, for whom it has brought a measure of financial independence in what is still a very male-dominated society. The seaweed is "planted" by tying it to ropes that are then staked in rows in the shallow intertidal zone of the lagoons, before being harvested and dried for a week, when it turns beautiful shades of russet, purple, green, mustard and blue.

21.838384, -78.763561

**CIEGO DE AVILA,
CUBA**

Private enterprise in Cuba, with all the strict rules and regulations that govern it, expresses itself in some pretty novel ways. Small-scale businesses, whose impact on state control of the economy is all but insignificant, have flourished in the jamboree of street-side vendors found in neighbourhoods across the land. The most common are the front-room caterers, the Cuban answer to the local candy store or mobile café, churning out everything from cakes and peanut bars to pizzas and sandwiches. Understanding the need to extend the life of replaceable items, enterprising businesspeople have developed roaring trades in cigarette lighter refuelling, watch mending and shoe-cleaning.

35.870736, 128.603328
**DAEGU,
KOREA**

A good place to sample the saccharine delights of present-day Korea, Daegu has developed into one large shopping mall, its city centre crisscrossed by streets devoted to particular products. Herbal Medicine Street is the best known – the city has for centuries been renowned for its natural remedies – but you can also head to Steamed Rib-Meat Street or Rice Cake Street if you're hungry, Shoe Street or Sock Street if your feet need clothing, or Washing Machine Appliance Street if, well, your washing machine needs maintenance. However, in a country obsessed with appearance, Daegu's main interest is the legendary beauty of its women; the city is based in a geological bowl, which makes for very hot summers, very cold winters and very delicious apples – the fruit that thrives in the surrounding countryside is said to keep the skin pimple-free, as well as providing the blanching effect that all Korean girls crave.

-22.951804, -43.211578
**LAGOA RODRIGO DE FREITAS,
RIO DE JANEIRO, BRAZIL**

Sitting pretty on the western shores of near-landlocked Guanabara Bay, no other city in the world can compete with Rio's sensational combination of urban sprawl, sandy shoreline and jungle-clad mountains. The city's streets and buildings have been moulded around the mountain range, while out in the bay, rocky islands are fringed with white sand. Even the concrete skyscrapers that dominate the skyline manage to look magnificent against their verdant backdrop – no wonder Rio's ten-million-strong citizens call it the Cidade Maravilhosa.

31.62587, -7.989646

**JEMMA EL FNA,
MARRAKECH, MOROCCO**

By day, Marrakech's central square – though fascinating for tourists – is resolutely Moroccan territory: no tourist is going to have a tooth pulled by one of the dentists here, no matter how neat the piles of molars displayed. Nor are you likely to use the scribes, street barbers or herb doctors, or, above all, understand the convoluted tales of the storytellers, around whom are gathered the most animated crowds in the square. More for tourists' benefit are the acrobats, who thrust forward into multiple somersaults and contortions in the late afternoon heat, and the sad-looking trained monkeys and snake charmers. In the evening, these give way to the Djemaa's enduring sound – dozens of musicians playing all kinds of instruments. As dusk falls, the square becomes a huge open-air, lantern-lit dining area, packed with stalls which send plumes of cooking smoke spiralling up into the night. The makeshift lanes of stalls have endless variety, selling everything from couscous and spicy merguez sausages to stewed snails and sheep's heads.

25.790989, 120.684814

**MATZU FERRY,
TAIWAN**

These days, guarding the shores of the Matzu Islands – thinly inhabited rocky outcrops of Taiwan just 16km off the coast of China – can be a little lacking in excitement. Despite being one of the most heavily militarized zones in the world, the Taiwanese conscripts sent to guard the islands are more likely to have their pictures taken by gawking tourists than face off against the People's Liberation Army. Since martial law was lifted in 1987, several former military installations have been opened for tours, and local residents are even allowed to engage in direct trade and travel with mainland China. It wasn't always like this. In the 1950s, Chiang Kai-shek's Nationalist forces fought ferocious battles with Mao's communists here, and Chinese bombardments continued well into the 1970s. Though the threat of war remains – China regards Taiwan as a "renegade province" – both sides have worked hard to maintain the peace, and tours of duty on Matzu are largely uneventful. Still, most soldiers here would rather be snoozing on duty than at war.

41.034885, 28.978001
NEVIZADE SOKAK, BEYOGLU, ISTANBUL, TURKEY

With a population estimated at anything up to 25 million, Istanbul is a metropolis going on megalopolis, a teeming, vibrant urban centre that can make other European cities seem dull in comparison – not least because it has a far younger age-profile than any EU city. It may have been stripped of its capital status back in 1923, but Istanbul still exerts a powerful, almost mystical hold on the psyche of the nation. There's a buzz and confidence in the air that makes everything and anything seem possible – and nowhere is this more palpable than in the Balik Pazarı (Fish Market). Hordes of Istanbullu hit the area at weekends, to gorge on heaps of meze and fish specialities and down copious amounts of rakı in rowdy *meyhanes* (taverns), before singing and dancing along to roving bands of Roma musicians.

35.628632, 139.738905

**SHINAGAWA STATION,
TOKYO, JAPAN**

When the morning rush hour hits Shinagawa station, it takes a certain amount of courage to go against the current. What starts as a trickle of bleary-eyed commuters soon becomes a great river of suits, flowing efficiently through the station's main corridor. And as the clock ticks closer to 9am, the migration gathers pace, forcing dissidents to walk along the edges of the crowd. It's strangely quiet though, and no matter how busy it gets, the river flows on. Huge yellow signs guide workers down from train platforms and into the station's stark central channel. From there, ramps and staircases filter them out onto the shimmering streets of Tokyo. It's here, in enormous glass towers, that thousands of salarymen and women carve out their names – and often a job for life – at some of Japan's biggest corporations. The hours can be brutal, and following the herd is vital for success. That's why the evening commute starts so slowly. But once the first few people leave their desks, the floodgates begin to creak open. Queues gradually form at coffee stands and people start pushing back towards the trains. For the next few hours, your safest bet is to go with the flow.

10.079581, 77.055573

**KERALA,
INDIA**

India's undisputed national drink is tea, or *chai*, grown on the border of Kerala and Tamil Nadu. Rising to well over 2500m, the wooded mountains here offer optimal conditions for tea cultivation, as the British were quick to discover. Vast swathes of virgin teak forest were clear-felled in the late nineteenth century to make way for plantations, and the hillsides here still support a giant patchwork of neatly cropped tea estates, interspersed with fragrant coffee and cardamom groves. Tea-picking is carried out by hand, usually by groups of women, whose dextrous fingers pick only the bud and first two leaves of each shoot before dropping them in a basket slung behind their backs. Despite the downturn in world consumption, Kerala's estates – the majority of them owned by the Indian multinational Tata – continue to churn out quantities of "CTC" ("cut, curl and trimmed") tea powder for the voracious domestic market.

Food and drink

Walking into the Dry Martini bar was a bit like going back in time: the style, the ambience, the soft golden light. Once I'd explained I was in Barcelona to take photos for Rough Guides, I was assured that the barman was the best Martini-mixer in Europe. He was great to photograph, with charisma and a passion for his craft, playing his role perfectly to help create some fantastic shots.

Chris Christoforou, *Photographer for The Rough Guide to Barcelona*

41.392728, 2.154091
**DRY MARTINI BAR,
BARCELONA**

Whatever you're looking for from a night out – bohemian boozer, underground club, cocktail bar, summer dance palace, techno temple, Irish pub or designer bar – you'll find it in Barcelona. If all you want is a drink, then any café or bar can oblige – but here, it's all about the specialist bars, with a plentiful choice of *bodegas* (specializing in wine), "pubs" and *cerveserías* (beer), *xampanyerías* (champagne and cava) and *coctelerías* (cocktails). For the latter, look no further than the legendary Dry Martini: with its white-jacketed bartenders, dark wood and brass, and expertly mixed drinks, it's the city's uptown cocktail bar par excellence.

14.942857, -91.111679
**CHICHICASTENANGO,
GUATEMALA**

Twice a week, the highland calm of Chichicastenango
in central Guatemala is shattered by the town's bustling
markets, which attract a myriad of day-tripping tourists and
commercial traders. The choice is overwhelming, ranging
from superb-quality Ixil clothing to wooden dance-masks
and everything in between, including lush, burstingly ripe
fruit and vegetables. For a great vantage point over the
vegetable market, head for the indoor balcony on the upper
floor of the Centro Comercial building. You'll be able to
gawk at the villagers below (as well as take photos without
fear of being intrusive) as they haggle and chat over
bunches of vegetables.

31.510875, -9.772215
**ESSAOUIRA,
MOROCCO**

The laid-back beach town of Essaouira is also an active
fishing port, and the harbour area bustles with life for most
of the day, with blue-and-white-ribbed boats being built or
repaired, and the fishing fleet bringing in the day's catch.
Just outside the port area is a line of fish grill-cafés, with
wooden tables and benches overlooking the main square
– an Essaouira institution. After a stroll along the harbour's
sun-bleached planks, there's no better place to snack on
sardines and other fish, freshly caught and grilled to sizzling
perfection in front of you.

22.282212, 114.155567
**LUK YU TEAHOUSE,
HONG KONG, CHINA**

The Luk Yu Teahouse is a Hong Kong highlight, famed for its antique interior and the quality of its dim sum – a breakfast of bite-sized dumplings and snacks served with tea. After settling into your wood-panelled booth, the first thing to do is to pick a brew: dark, smoky *bo lei* is the favourite with Hong Kongers to counteract the impact of the rich food, but the more delicate *tiet kwun yam* ("Iron Buddha") works well too. Then it's time to work through the menu cards provided, ticking off your choices as you sort through the mind-boggling array of options. But understanding the menu isn't always easy, even if you can read Chinese: "red bean sand soup" turns out to be a sweet porridge of adzuki bean puree, and the exotic-sounding "phoenix claws" are actually a considerably less enticing plate of steamed chicken's feet. Finally, the waiters glide over with your selection steaming away inside little bamboo baskets: paper-thin *sheung fan*, rice-flour rolls stuffed with crunchy prawns; transparent-skinned *har gau* dumplings, tinted pink by their shrimp and bamboo-shoot stuffing; a plate of fragrant roast duck; and some astringent, dark-green kale dressed in soy sauce and peanut oil.

-34.553358, -58.436741
**SUCRE, BELGRANO,
BUENOS AIRES, ARGENTINA**

Buenos Aires has firmly established itself as Latin America's gastronomic capital – São Paulo may rival it for variety, but nowhere else on the continent can touch it for quality. The mainstay of Porteño cuisine is the barbecue, or *parrilla*, and the crowning glory of most menus are, of course, the beautiful cuts of world-famous beef delivered daily from the city's hinterland. But alongside traditional cooking, the city has an evolving bon vivant (*buen vivir*) culture, which in recent years has seen palates grow finer, the clientele become more exacting and chefs make greater use of the fresh produce at their disposal; haute cuisine (*cocina de autor*) is now a well-established part of the city's culinary landscape.

51.506859, -0.141943
**THE RITZ, LONDON,
UK**

With its extravagant Louis XVI interiors and air of luxury, The Ritz hotel has been a byword for decadence since it first wowed Edwardian society in 1906. You can always linger outside to gawp at the fur-coat-clad dowagers and dapper gents that cross the hallowed threshold – but it's much more fun to join them inside. You'll need to be well dressed (jacket and tie for men), have a good appetite, and book in advance for the famous afternoon tea in the hotel's Palm Court. Amid the chink of silver spoons in fine china teacups and the hum of polite chit-chat, you can feast on dainty sandwiches and lashings of scones with cream, not to mention all manner of fancy cakes.

26.206463, 73.064693
**RAJASTHAN,
INDIA**

If going solo in rural Rajasthan seems daunting, sign up for a "village safari" to take you to the heart of a Bishnoi village, where you can watch crafts such as spinning and carpet-making, taste traditional food – and try opium tea. During the opium ceremony, the drug is dissolved in water in a specially designed wooden vessel, and poured through a strainer into a second receptacle. The process is repeated twice more, and the resulting tea is drunk from the palm of a hand. Strictly speaking, it's illegal, but blind eyes are turned to this kind of traditional opium use – even though opium addiction is something of a social problem in rural Rajasthan.

18.378169, -65.716280

**KIOSCOS,
PUERTO RICO**

Traditional Puerto Rican food, known as *cocina criolla*, is firmly rooted in simple but tasty Spanish cuisine, and heavily influenced by the island's Taíno and African inhabitants. It's certainly no-frills – served up on paper plates, at the beach or off the road – but the spit-roasted meats, fresh seafood and crispy fritters are tantalizing nonetheless, washed down with fine mountain coffee and the best rum in the Caribbean. One of Puerto Rico's purest pleasures is spending an afternoon trawling *kioscos*, simple shacks that knock out mouthwatering fritters, *pinchos* (kebabs) and slabs of seafood for a handful of change. The *kioscos* along the east coast are particularly tempting, with a ready supply of fresh fish: *pastelillos* (deep-fried turnovers) stuffed with trunkfish or shark meat turn lunch into a feast.

40.721569, -73.995616
LOMBARDI'S, NEW YORK CITY, USA

Ask a dozen New Yorkers which of the city's innumerable pizzerias serves up the best slice and you'll get a dozen different (and vociferous) answers. None would dispute Lombardi's status as the grande signora of New York's pizza parlours, however. America's oldest pizzeria first opened in 1905, when Gennaro Lombardi began firing up his celebrated coal oven in the family grocery store to feed Little Italy's burgeoning immigrant population. Passed down through generations of Lombardis, it has spawned its own extended family as well as countless imitators, but has maintained its loyal following with the consistency of its delicately charred thin-crust pies, made in the Neapolitan tradition. And despite closing in 1984 and popping up a decade later at its current location just down the street, the crowds have never wavered. There's invariably a wait, but those in the know stick it out for the clam pies, topped with fresh clams, garlic and just enough olive oil and pecorino romano cheese to dispense with any traditional sauce.

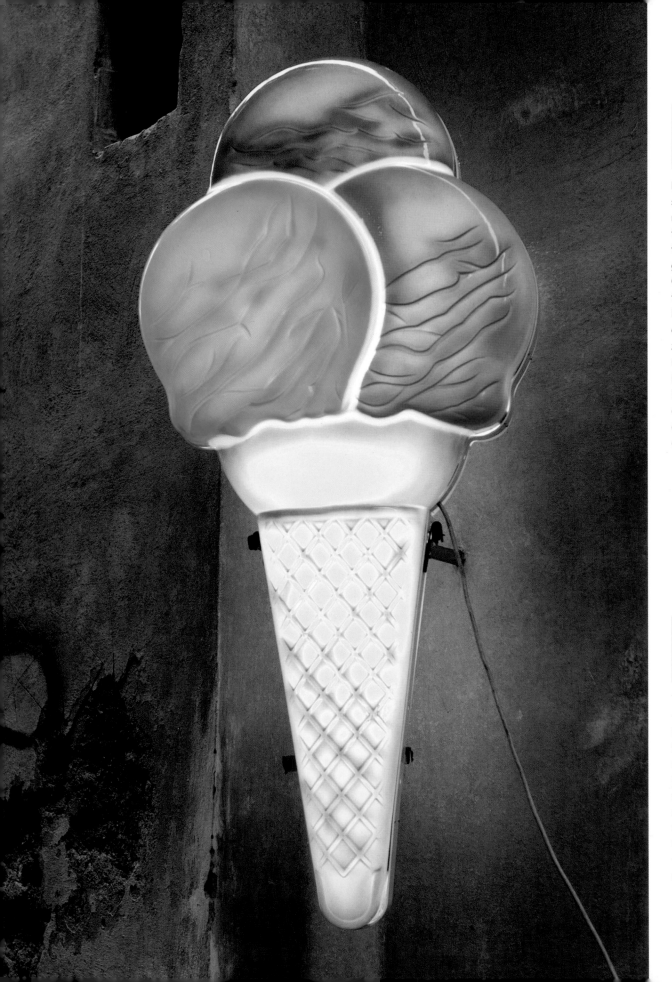

41.901481, 12.484957
**ROME,
ITALY**

Forget the multi-flavoured transatlantic imitators: Italy is still home to the best ice cream in the world. Granted, it's not all first-rate, but in Rome, you'd be hard-pressed to find substandard gelato anywhere. In the last few years, the quality of the raw ingredients has become key to the gelateria's success. The brothers behind the legendary San Crispino founded their enormously successful gelateria in the early 1990s, and take their craft very seriously indeed. Ingredients are of a luxuriously high quality: only 20-year-old Marsala from a Sicilian winery will do for their trademark zabaione flavour; the ice cream is stored in silver canisters, rather than plastic tubs; and cones are banned, as anything but a paper cup will taint the delicate flavours. Every Roman has his own view on the true *crème de la crème* of ice-cream parlours; ask around, or be guided by the crowds of gelato-guzzling locals outside – a sure-fire sign of ice-cream heaven.

48.133301, 11.549334
**OKTOBERFEST, MUNICH,
GERMANY**

The single most important thing to know about Oktoberfest – Munich's legendary festival of beer and bonhomie – is that the bulk of the Fest generally takes place during the last two weeks in September. Predictably enough, massive and widespread public drunkenness is a regular phenomenon – some seven million visitors manage to down over four million litres of beer in just sixteen days – which doesn't stop the revellers from visiting the enormous funfair that runs alongside the beer tents. One additional annual ritual is the intake of breath at the price of a *Mass* of beer – it may be good, but carousing Oktoberfest-style certainly doesn't come cheap.

52.35605, 4.877157
CAFE WELLING, AMSTERDAM, THE NETHERLANDS

The Dutch concept of *gezellig* doesn't translate itself easily into English. It's a cocktail of cosiness, friendliness, informal acceptance and companionship, and sums up the special ethos of the city perfectly. A lingering summer picnic in the Vondelpark; a rainy afternoon spent in one of Amsterdam's 200 coffee shops with friends and a plateful of chocolate-chip-and-hash cookies; watching ice-skaters on the frozen canals under twinkling lights; all can produce that intangible state of *gezelligheid* that defines this city. But the traditional home of *gezellig*, so to speak, is the *bruin* café (so called because years of smoke and spilled beer have stained these typical Dutch drinking holes a characteristic brown), where affable Dutch sociability comes into its own. Sample some of the Netherlands finest pilsners and set the world to rights over a long afternoon, as Amsterdammers have done since the Golden Age.

16.461110, 107.587770
STREET FOOD, HUE, VIETNAM

From hawkers with cauldrons of soup dangling from shoulder poles, to pushcarts, market stalls and makeshift "street kitchens", Vietnam's street-food scene is unsurpassed. Though the choice is enormous, most vendors are highly specialized, serving one type of food or even just a single dish, but they cook it to perfection. All you need is a bit of judicious selection – look for places with a fast turnover, where the ingredients are obviously fresh – then dig in. Thanks to a varied topography and climate, Vietnam's cooks have an unusually broad range of ingredients to call on, from temperate fruits and vegetables grown in the cool uplands to the tropical bounty of the Mekong Delta, so you'll find a great deal of regional variation in the food on offer: northern dishes include hotpots, rice gruels and sweet-and-sour soups, while southern flavours feature curries and spicy dipping sauces. Tet, the Vietnamese New Year, is the pinnacle of the street-food calendar, when vendors go into overdrive as everyone snacks to their hearts' content.

17.963161, 102.604918
**VIENTIANE,
LAOS**

Set on a broad curve of the Mekong, Vientiane is perhaps Southeast Asia's most modest capital city. Though it may lack the buzz of Ho Chi Minh City or Bangkok, Laos's capital has been transformed in recent years from a desolate city of boarded-up shopfronts into a quaint backwater, with a string of cosmopolitan restaurants and cafés. It's a place for kicking back for a few days and taking life at a Lao pace – epitomized by sunset drinks on the banks of the Mekong and tasty, home-style cooking. Riverside food stalls along the Mekong offer staples like *tam màk hung* (spicy papaya salad), *pîng kai* (grilled chicken) and crusty baguettes (*khào jì*) filled with Lao-style pâté, Vientiane's speciality snack.

48.858143, 2.272282
LA GARE, PARIS, FRANCE

Most visitors come to Paris with an appetite, and high expectations. This is, after all, the city that invented the concept of the restaurant, and indeed of fine cooking. But while the city's celebrity art-chefs relentlessly pursue culinary perfection, and the avant-garde pacesetters operate at the very cutting edge of gastronomy, the cuisine at the average Parisian restaurant or simpler, more local bistrot is surprisingly conservative. In a recent survey, more than two-thirds of French people named a simple steak-frites as their favourite dish, and out of the almost ten thousand restaurants in the city, almost ninety percent feature primarily French cooking, with quality and precision valued over inventiveness and experimentation.

**DAZHALAN STREET TEA SHOP,
BEIJING, CHINA**

Tea has been central to the Chinese way of life for more than 4000 years; even the traditional wedding ceremony involves bonding over shared cups. A staple of every meal, it's brewed in hot – not boiling – water and, of course, drunk straight, without milk or sugar. Tea made in the correct way, usually at formal occasions, is something of an art form: first, all the teaware is washed with boiling water; the pot is then lined with tea leaves and a quick first brew made and thrown away – just to rinse the leaves; finally, the second brew is poured into a tiny cup. The type of pot too, is important; the most celebrated are made from the purplish clay from Yixing in Jiangsu Province. These pots are unglazed, so slightly porous. After years of use, a patina develops on the interior which, it is said, enhances the taste of any tea steeped inside.

40.722340, -73.987291

**KATZ'S, NEW YORK CITY,
USA**

New York's legendary deli, Katz's, was opened in the Lower East Side by a Russian immigrant family in 1888. In the early twentieth century, it quickly established itself as a reliable supplier of pickles and salami to the Lower East Side's newly emigrated masses. Now it's perhaps the world's most famous deli, and even frazzled New Yorkers don't mind waiting in line for its overstuffed pastrami or corned-beef sandwiches. Doused with mustard and complemented by a side pile of pickles, one of these should keep you going for about a week.

13.721276, 100.517730

LEBUA, BANGKOK, THAILAND

Bangkok boasts an astonishing fifty thousand places to eat – that's almost one for every hundred citizens – ranging from grubby street-side noodle shops to the most elegant of restaurants. If you've had your fill of Thai street food, treat yourself to a taste of the high life: even if you don't splurge on one of the Lebua hotel's extravagant suites, you can still mingle with the smart set at its rooftop Sky Bar, a standing-room-only roost above the city. Come around 6pm to take in the stunning, near-360° panoramas as day blends into night, with a pricey cocktail in hand. Also up here is Mediterranean Sirocco, which has the distinction of being the world's highest alfresco restaurant, at 275m above the pavements of Bangkok – but with views this spectacular, you'll hardly notice what's on your plate.

41.034549, 28.979809

**SARAY PATISSERIE,
ISTANBUL, TURKEY**

Istiklal Caddesi (Independence Street) is Istanbul's most exciting thoroughfare, with a vibrant, almost hedonistic atmosphere that makes it quite distinct from anywhere else in the city – locals come here in droves to shop, wine and dine, take in a film, club or gig, or simply stroll. Perfectly placed to draw the crowds of hungry promenaders, upmarket patisserie Saray has been famed for its Turkish delicacies since it opened in 1935. As well as mouthwatering profiteroles, it's a sure bet for classic desserts such as *fırın sütlaç* (baked rice pudding) and *irmik helvası* (semolina with nuts), as well as baklava-type sweets – the sticky, syrupy heaps in the window are a siren call to sweet-toothed Istanbullu.

Keepsakes

Photographing hill tribes and ethnic minority groups in Southeast Asia is never easy, but some of my favourite pictures have been of these amazing peoples. Local markets are always lively and full of energy, and make fantastic pictures. Showing genuine interest in somebody's work – such as these wonderful dolls – before removing a camera from its case is an often-overlooked way of reassuring people who are unused to having their photo taken.

Tim Draper, *Photographer for The Rough Guide to Laos*

19.895766, 102.143197
**TRIBAL MARKET,
LOUANG PHABANG, LAOS**

As the sun slinks down into the mountains, casting a heavy glow over Laos' ancient capital, hundreds of crimson sheets are unfurled onto the pavements. Villagers from across the region quickly unpack their wares, setting the main street ablaze with colour, and Louang Phabang's famous tribal market is open for business. It's here, down by the river, that you'll find jars of snake wine lined up on the floor. There are rows of ornate stone Buddhas and great bundles of sickly sweet incense waiting to go up in smoke. But it's in the quietest corner of the market, lit by a single electric bulb, that you'll come across some of Laos' most popular souvenirs: these extraordinary dolls, painstakingly pieced together in a colourful tribute to the country's ethnic diversity. Each of the dazzling costumes signifies a different tribal group, and local materials are used to ensure complete authenticity. Among the bestselling pieces are those that represent the Akha hill tribe; their bejewelled headdresses and dark blue pantaloons make them stand out from the crowd, but most market-goers still have difficulty deciding on a single doll. No wonder, then, that so many of them come away with a handful.

23.165910, -81.230421
**VARADERO,
CUBA**

Varadero is *the* package resort in Cuba, a giant playground of large-scale resort hotels spread across a 25km-long peninsula that protrudes like a fingertip from the north coast of the island. The golden carpet of fine sand bathed by placid emerald-green waters is almost the perfect vision of a tropical paradise; indeed, before the Revolution, this was one of the most renowned, modern and hedonistic holiday spots in the Caribbean. Castro's hostility to tourism changed much of that, but things have been on the upswing since the 1990s. Despite the signs of burgeoning tourism – from the spread of luxury hotels to the hawkers peddling souvenirs on the beach – a lingering legacy of peeling shopfronts and down-at-heel restaurants and clubs keep Varadero peculiarly and defiantly Cuban.

48.903313, 2.339154
**ST-OUEN, PARIS,
FRANCE**

It's easy to lose track of an entire morning browsing the acres of fine antiques, covetable curios and general bric-a-brac at St-Ouen, the mother of Paris's flea markets. It's come a long way from the days when secondhand mattresses, clothes and other infested junk were sold here in a free-for-all zone outside the city walls. Nowadays, it's predominantly a proper – and very expensive – antiques market, with over a dozen separate sections covering some two thousand shops. To better your chances of finding something you could feasibly carry home, head for Marché Vernaison, the oldest in the complex, and the closest thing to a real flea market. Its maze-like, creeper-covered alleys are fun to wander along, threading your way between stalls selling all manner of bric-a-brac. Marché Jules-Vallès is smaller but similar, stuffed with books and records, vintage clothing, colonial knick-knacks and other curiosities, while Marché Dauphine shelters an eclectic mix of decorative antique furniture, vintage fashions and rare books.

35.700398, 139.771321
**AKIHABARA,
TOKYO, JAPAN**

The Japanese crush their way through seventeen billion cans each year. That might sound like a lot, but when you consider the sheer variety of things squeezed into them and sold by machines on the streets of Tokyo, it's hardly surprising. Of course there are the usuals – Coke, iced tea and orange juice – but you can just as easily pick up a can of hot coffee or an ice-cold beer as you make your way through the city. There are canned snacks, too – like this bread, protected from the outside world by its shiny anime armour. All of these treats are just a pocketful of change away, thanks to Japan's enduring obsession with the vending machine. It's estimated there's one of these robo-shops for every 23 people in the country, and almost every imaginable need is catered for. There are machines that sell umbrellas. Others lay fresh eggs, like giant mechanical chickens. And, if you know where to look, you'll find fishing bait and pot plants are available at the press of a button. When you're travelling in Tokyo, the best advice is to look after your spare change – you can never be quite sure when you'll need it.

11.155667, -60.839860
**STORE BAY BEACH,
TOBAGO**

Only a two-minute walk from Tobago's dinky airport, Store Bay Beach is what most people come to the island for: powdery sand, crystal-clear water, a chilled-out vibe and good food, with all-you-can-eat beach barbecues cranking up the volume in high season, and vast quantities of curry crab and dumplin' at any time of the year. When you're done with lazing and eating, check out the craft stalls that line the beach – home to some of the most colourful souvenirs you'll find in the Caribbean.

25.220457, 55.280156
CROWNE PLAZA, DUBAI, UNITED ARAB EMIRATES

International brands – from Marks & Spencer to Armani – may have taken a firm grip of much of Dubai's retail trade, but there are still plenty of authentically Arabian souvenirs to look out for too. You can shop for everything from authentic antique Omani silverware to tacky belly-dancing costumes – not to mention the huge trade in fake designer clothing and accessories for which the city remains famous. And those with cash to burn head to the glittering Gold Souk, where dazzled western tourists rub shoulders with Indian and African traders in search of a bargain. Dubai is also one of the best places in the world to go shopping for carpets, with innumerable outlets offering rugs from all over Asia – anything from museum-quality Persian heirlooms to inexpensive prayer mats and kilims.

13.758965,100.497166
BANGLAMPHU, BANGKOK, THAILAND

Most of the swarms of budget travellers that descend on Bangkok head straight for Banglamphu, the city's long-established travellers' ghetto, where if you're not careful you could end up watching DVDs all day long and selling your shoes when you run out of money. At the heart of the district is the legendary Thanon Khao San, almost a caricature of a travellers' centre: a lively, high-energy place, it's crammed with internet cafés, dodgy travel agents, tattooists and hair-braiders, its pavements lined with stalls flogging cheap backpackers' fashions, racks of bootleg CDs and kitschy Thai souvenirs.

14.372185, 100.541816
**WAT PHU KHAO TONG,
AYUTTHAYA, THAILAND**

Fortunes are made and lost over cock fights in Thailand: it makes no difference that it's illegal to bet on this strange, brutal sport, in which the birds, pumped up on amphetamines and steroids, peck each other into squawking submission. The stakes couldn't have been higher, though, in the legendary sixteenth-century cock fight between the young Burmese Crown Prince and his peer, Naresuan, hostage son of the vassal Thai king. As immortalized in countless stories, temple murals and even a blockbuster biopic, Prince Naresuan restored national pride first by winning the royal cock fight and then by clawing back the Thai kingdom of Ayutthaya, repelling the Burmese invaders and installing himself as monarch. A colossal statue of King Naresuan the Great now presides over the approach to the Ayutthayan temple of Wat Phu Khao Tong. He is on horseback, surrounded by the massed statues of scores of white-tailed cockerels, a fighting breed famous for its endurance and pluck.

37.381839, -6.007889
**SEVILLE,
SPAIN**

Twenty-five years or so ago, flamenco was on the decline, preserved only in the clubs of its aficionados, or in travestied castanet-clicking form for tourists. But Spain's richest musical heritage went through a tremendous period of innovation in the 1980s and 90s, incorporating elements of pop, rock, jazz and Latin, and today there's a new respect for the old "pure flamenco" artists, and a huge joy in the new. The music was thought to have been brought to Spain by gypsies in the fifteenth century, and flamenco still tends to thrive in quarters of gitano and refugee origin, such as the Triana barrio of Seville, where, as well as watching a performance of the hand-clapping, finger-snapping dance, you can pick up souvenirs such as these flouncy-skirted flamenco aprons.

37.796081, -122.406722
**CHINATOWN, SAN FRANCISCO,
CALIFORNIA, USA**

San Francisco is home to one of the largest Chinese communities outside Asia. As Chinatown grows, its diversity increases, adding Taiwanese, Vietnamese, Korean, Thai, and Laotian families to the mix; the cultural fusion is most evident in grocery stores, where alongside traditional Chinese produce, you'll see Italian basil, Mexican kohlrabi bulbs, and Vietnamese vegetables. The Chinatown Gate makes a suitably dramatic entrance to the area. Facing south, as per feng shui precepts, this large dragon-clad arch leads to sidewalks paved with plastic Buddhas, noisemakers and chirping mechanical crickets that assault the ear and eye from every doorway.

23.141884, -82.351483

**HAVANA,
CUBA**

The markets of Old Havana are knee-deep in Che Guevara memorabilia, vintage American car paintings and cigar-themed nonsense, but occasionally a cool piece catches the eye. Fantastic paintings and prints, lacquered puffer fish, pumpkin-seed necklaces, handmade leather items and these colourful clay figurines are just some of the wares on offer. There are some more offbeat souvenirs too: what price a transcript of one of Fidel Castro's day-long speeches?

43.657091, -70.253507
PORTLAND,
MAINE, USA

The sea looms large in the history of Maine, eastern USA's most northerly state – with a wild and thinly populated hinterland, it's the ocean that has sustained its population since the first colonies were established here in the seventeenth century. Though fishing and shipbuilding remain important, tourism plays an increasingly crucial role in Maine's economy. Not surprisingly, nautical antique stores are a speciality, with brass lanterns, barometers, telescopes, ship's compasses, scrimshaw and ship carvings all enthusiastically collected. Perhaps the most sought-after objects are the carved figureheads that once graced the clipper ships of the nineteenth century, many created in the state. The figurehead symbolized the spirit of a ship and was believed to appease the gods of the sea and ensure a safe voyage. The most popular form was a female figure, often mermaids or what the sailors considered "exotic" totems – an Indian princess or Polynesian maiden. Even actresses were honoured: images of Jenny Lind, the "Swedish Nightingale" who wowed US audiences in the 1850s, adorned many a Maine-built ship and are now collector's items.

-13.420992, -71.850087
**SACRED VALLEY,
PERU**

A vital Inca road once snaked its way up the canyon that enters the Sacred Valley at Pisac in southern Peru, and ancient Incan traditions still persist to this day. The thriving morning market in the town's main square is a good place to pick up local souvenirs such as hand-painted ceramic beads and these woven papoose dolls. Andean textiles and weaves have been a part of village life for more than two thousand years here. Weavers still use the techniques and designs pioneered by their ancestors, passing them on to their children, who first sit down at the loom at six or seven years old.

31.627935, -7.988284

MARRAKECH, MOROCCO

Morocco is big on crafts, and pretty much every part of the country has its speciality. The covered, atmospheric souks of Marrakech seem vast the first time you venture in, and almost impossible to navigate, though in fact the area that they cover is pretty compact, with different sections specializing in different goods, from furniture to ironwork, slippers and musical instruments. The best place to buy carpets is, naturally enough, the carpet souk, and there are souks for jewellery, for *babouches* (Moroccan slippers), for spices – and just about anything else that you could conceivably want to parcel up and take home, including 'silverware' made from old tyres.

18.785076, 99.000233

CHIANG MAI, THAILAND

Shopping is an almost irresistible pastime in Chiang Mai, a hotbed of traditional cottage industries offering high standards of workmanship at bargain-basement prices. Two main shopping areas, the San Kamphaeng road and the night bazaar, sell the full range of local handicrafts: you can pick up everything from prized local silks and carved wooden elephants to mulberry paper and lacquerware. The sprawling night bazaar is a shopper's playground, with bumper-to-bumper street stalls and several indoor market areas and multistorey arcades, which sell just about anything produced in Chiang Mai, plus crafts from other parts of Thailand and Southeast Asia, as well as the obligatory counterfeit designer gear.

**PANJIAYUAN ANTIQUES
MARKET, BEIJING, CHINA**

There's no shortage of antique stores and markets in China's capital, offering opium pipes, jade statues, porcelain Mao figurines, mahjong sets, Red Guard alarm clocks, Fu Manchu glasses, and all manner of bric-a-brac – pretty much all of it fake. The jade is actually soapstone, inset jewels are glass, and that venerable painting is a print stained with tea. So long as you're not browsing for heirlooms, Panjiayuan – also called the "Dirt Market" – is a good place to head, with a vast range of souvenirs and secondhand goods for sale; among the junk, you'll find decently priced traditional souvenirs such as seals, kites, papercuts (images cut into thin card), tea sets and ornamental chopsticks.

**VENICE,
ITALY**

Venice was once famed as a place in which almost anything could be bought or sold, and it's still a thriving commercial city – in the sense that its shops rake in millions of euros every day from the visiting throngs. Nowadays, though, the great majority of the glitzy emporia in the main retail areas are not Venetian, but the outposts of the same big-gun Italian designer brands you'll find in any tourist hotspot. With each passing year and rent increase, the smaller-scale Venetian enterprises are finding it harder to compete, though many authentic outlets and workshops are still to be found away from the main drags. The manufacture of beautiful decorative papers is a distinctively Venetian skill; small craft studios continue to produce covetable handmade bags and shoes; and there are plenty of shops selling glass, lace and Carnival masks – even if the fakes greatly outnumber the genuine articles.

Nature

Though a jaguar in Guatemala was on my photo-shoot list, I knew that running into one would be a near impossibility. But after photographing the birds at a nature reserve in Flores, one of the employees asked if I would like to see a jaguar that had been rescued from a forest fire as a baby a few years before. We walked to the compound where it was sleeping just centimetres away, with only a thin fence separating us. As I lifted my camera up to the wire it suddenly woke, turned, snarled and attacked, leaping full force at the fence and catapulting me from my crouched position two metres into the air. I got this shot the moment before the jaguar hit the fence.

Tim Draper, Photographer for The Rough Guide to Guatemala

16.928910, -89.873829
FLORES, PETÉN, GUATEMALA

The vast northern department of Petén occupies about a third of Guatemala but contains just over three percent of its population. This expanse of tropical rainforest, swamp and savannah stretches into southern Mexico and across the Maya Mountains to Belize, and huge tracts remain virtually untouched. Ancient mahogany trees tower 50m above the forest floor, sheltering an extraordinarily rich variety of wildlife – hummingbirds, toucans, buzzards, wild turkeys and birds of paradise, and, beneath the forest canopy, lumbering tapir, ocelots, deer, coatis and jaguars. Sadly, this jungle paradise is under threat: waves of settlers have cleared enormous sections, and oil exploration and commercial logging have brought with them mountains of money and machinery, cutting new roads deep into the forest. Schemes such as UNESCO's biosphere reserves are an attempt to preserve what remains, and environmental groups are fighting to halt the relentless destruction of the rainforest.

-45.345083, 170.826116

**OTAGO,
NEW ZEALAND**

The Maori believed the large, grey and almost perfectly spherical Moeraki Boulders, on New Zealand's Otago coast, to be food baskets washed ashore from the shipwrecked canoe – in fact a boat-shaped seaward reef – you can see just offshore. These smooth domes of rock – some of them two metres in diameter – hunker on the sandy beach, partially submerged, and reveal honeycomb centres when broken. They were not in fact washed up by the sea, and nor did they fall from the sky, but in fact lay deep inside the mudstone cliffs behind the beach. As the sea eroded the cliffs, out fell the boulders; their distinctive fractured surface was formed as further erosion exposed a network of veins. There used to be many more of the boulders, strewn like oversized marbles along the shore, but most have been swiped by souvenir hunters, leaving only those too heavy to shift.

45.468318, 22.898254

**TRANSYLVANIA,
ROMANIA**

Thanks to Bram Stoker and Hollywood, Transylvania is most famous abroad as the haunt of Dracula, a mountainous place where storms lash medieval hamlets, while wolves – or werewolves – howl from the surrounding woods. The scenery is certainly dramatic, but it's the crisp, clean air and hushed beauty of the Retezat National Park in southern Transylvania that make you catch your breath. An idyllic landscape of lushly forested expanses and well-defined peaks, often reflected in clear alpine lakes, it's a far cry from the gothic landscape that Bram Stoker conjured up as the homeland of the ultimate horror icon.

37.942475, -119.027681
**CALIFORNIA,
USA**

The placid blue waters of the primordial Mono Lake are surrounded by volcanic desert, its two large islands lapped by salty, alkaline water, with numerous hot springs and freakish towers and spires formed by their deposits. Though in existence for around a million years, the lake is under threat by a place some 800km away – the city of Los Angeles, whose insatiable water demands are gradually draining it dry. The water levels here have dropped by around thirty metres over the past seventy years, menacing the resident birdlife, and even humans, with the winds blowing across the saltpans wafting arsenic-laced clouds across its ever more arid expanses. But help is at hand. Through government intervention and the work of local activists, the lake will still be there, with any luck, for another millennium at least.

44.653455, 1.477184
**DORDOGNE,
FRANCE**

The Dordogne has been seducing expats from Britain, Belgium and Holland for years, who swoon over its picturesque villages and unpopulated countryside and gorge on the local truffles, foie gras and fine wine. Historically and locally known as Perigord, the area is divided into four areas based on the colours that represent its most dominant natural features: white for its limestone plateaus and chalky soil, green for its verdant valleys, purple for its vineyards and black for its dark oak and dense pine forests – but you'd be forgiven for adding a fifth, yellow, for its sunflowers: Perigord's quintessential crop.

54.570499, -3.170757

CAT BELLS, LAKE DISTRICT, UK

The Lake District – wild, craggy and epic in scale – has a unique hold on British hearts. From Wordsworth and Coleridge onwards, it has appealed to that part of the nation's character that sees nothing more romantic than a windswept hike up a challenging hill. Cat Bells, high above the western shore of Derwentwater, has sweeping views of the verdant countryside of this damp northwestern corner of England. From Hawes End, a pier on Derwentwater, a path climbs sharply to ascend the 450m of Cat Bells; the curious name stems from a Norse belief that the hill was home to a den of wild cats. It's a steep scramble, but one that rewards you with a panorama of grand dimensions. And of course, this being England, you're never too far from a pint in a country pub; descending from Cat Bells, try the Swinside Inn, a short walk from Hawes End.

Sitting high above the Dordogne, the castle of Les Milandes, once owned by the cabaret artist and Folies Bergère star Josephine Baker, has all the necessary romantic ingredients: towers, balustrades, gargoyles, ornate dormer windows and terraced gardens shaded by great, glossy-leafed magnolias. After she bought Les Milandes in 1947, Josephine set about modernizing it, adding creature comforts such as the en-suite bathrooms, whose decor was inspired by her favourite perfumes – Arpège-style black tiles with gold taps and ceiling in one, Dioresque pink marble with silver-leaf in another. The falconry demonstrations held on the terrace are in keeping with the eccentricity of the place, and with Baker's love of animals: throughout her life, she was surrounded by menageries, sharing her dressing room with a goat called Toutoute and her kitchen with her pig, Albert, whom she doused with the perfume Je Reviens. Most famously, she was joined in her act at the Casino de Paris by a cheetah, Chiquita, which wore a diamond choker and accompanied her everywhere she went.

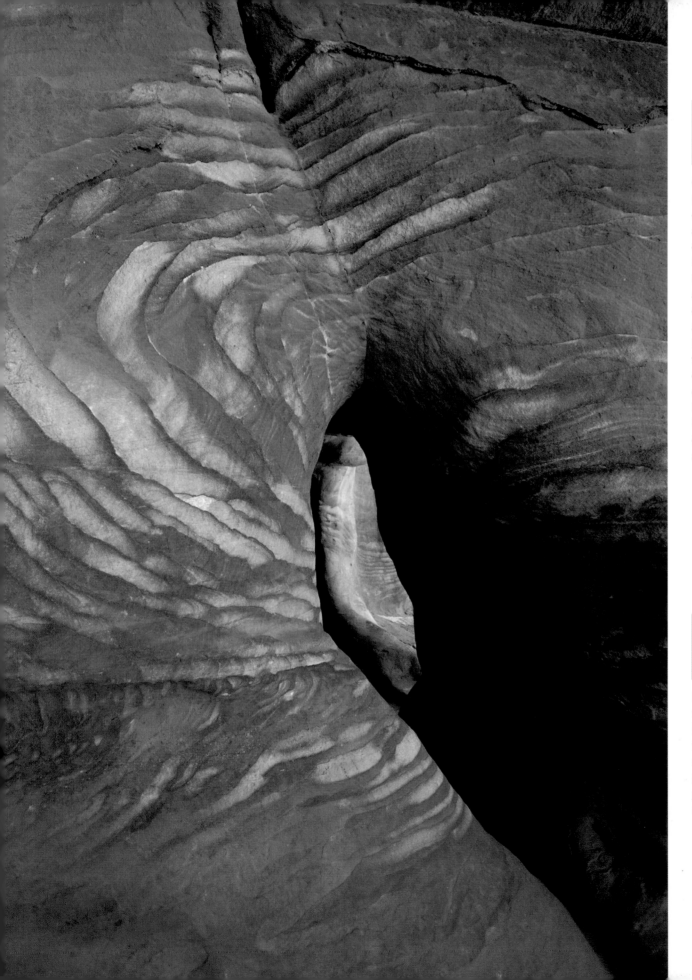

30.322936, 35.450971
**PETRA,
JORDAN**

One of the most breathtaking aspects of Petra – for many people surpassing even the architecture – is its colourful sandstone. Over the centuries, wind has rubbed away at the the cliffs to reveal an extraordinary array of colours streaking through the stone. When the artist Edward Lear strolled up the Colonnaded Street on a visit in 1858, coolly noting "the tint of the stone… brilliant and gay beyond my anticipation", his manservant and cook burst out in delight, "Oh master, we have come into a world of chocolate, ham, curry powder and salmon!" However, the most famous lines on Petra's colours were written by John William Burgon, later to become Dean of Chichester, in 1845, who described it as "A rose-red city half as old as Time". No advertising copywriter could have dreamt up a better line, and Burgon's trite slogan has since hung over Petra like a bad smell: you'll be sick of reading the words "rose-red city" on every map, poster and booklet by the time you leave.

41.508291, 8.910277
**GOLFE DE ROCCAPINA,
CORSICA, FRANCE**

Corsica boasts some of the cleanest and least-polluted waters in all the Mediterranean, with over 200 enticing beaches. The Golfe de Roccapina, a typically dazzling turquoise-blue bay, is a protected site whose dunes are empty but for a desultory municipal campsite. The area gets crowded from early July, but come off-season and you can have Roccapina's soft white sand and crystal-clear waters all to yourself.

34.041501, -116.100554
JOSHUA TREE NATIONAL PARK, CALIFORNIA, USA

The outdoors is one of California's treasures, and the state's fabulous parks come thick with superlatives: Sequoia National Park holds the largest trees in the world, Death Valley contains the lowest point in the Western Hemisphere, and both are rivalled by the extraordinary domes and spires of Yosemite. Serious desert enthusiasts should make a beeline for Joshua Tree National Park, a sublime place of crimson sunsets and weird cactus formations. Most cacti present few problems, but you should keep an eye out for the eight-foot cholla (pronounced "choy-uh"), or jumping cholla as some are called, because of the way segments seem to jump off and attach themselves to you if you brush past.

50.737638, 0.257986
**BEACHY HEAD,
SUSSEX, UK**

With nowhere in England more than 120km from the coast, the sea – bulwark against the Spanish Armada, Napoleon and Hitler – occupies an integral part of the English psyche. Poets, painters and photographers have been inspired through the centuries by the bays and beaches, cliffs and creeks, sand dunes and shingle of the country's diverse coastline. The stretch of coast that borders Sussex is one of the country's most iconic, its chalk uplands cut by the sea into a sequence of splendid cliffs. The most spectacular of all, Beachy Head, is 175m high, with a diminutive-looking lighthouse, but no beach – the headland's name derives from the French *beau chef* meaning "beautiful head". The beauty certainly went to the German philosopher Friedrich Engels' head; he insisted his ashes be scattered here, and depressed individuals regularly try to join him by leaping to their doom from this well-known suicide spot.

37.866323, 20.623312

**SHIPWRECK BAY,
ZÁKYNTHOS, GREECE**

The Ionian islands, shepherding their satellites down the west coast of mainland Greece, float on a haze of turquoise Ionian sea, their lush green silhouettes coming as a shock to those more used to the stark outlines of the Aegean. Although some of the islands sport a level of development to match the Spanish costas, there are still some beautifully secluded pockets to be discovered. Zákynthos is no exception: many of its beaches are towel-to-towel in high season, but if you rent a boat to potter around the coast, you can drop anchor at fantastically isolated spots like Shipwreck Bay, which still harbours the skeleton of a cargo ship that ran aground here in the 1960s.

9.979751, -83.847613
**PARQUE NACIONAL VOLCÁN
IRAZÚ, COSTA RICA**

The blasted lunar landscape of the Parque Nacional Volcán Irazú reaches its highest point at 3432m, on clear days offering fantastic views all the way to the Caribbean coast. Famous for having had the gall to erupt on the day President Kennedy visited the country on March 19, 1963, Irazú has been more or less calm ever since. But while it is less active in terms of bubblings and rumblings than the other volcanoes here, its deep crater and the algae-green lake that fills it create an undeniably dramatic sight. Looming 32km north of Cartago, the volcano makes for a long and entirely uphill but scenic trip, especially in the early morning before the inevitable clouds roll in. Up at the top you'll see very little vegetation, and what does grow has an otherworldly quality, struggling to survive in this strange environment.

17.016384, 99.701979

**SUKHOTHAI HISTORICAL
PARK, THAILAND**

Every year on the evening of the full moon of the twelfth lunar month (usually in November), Thais all over the country celebrate the end of the rainy season with the festival of Loy Krathong. One of Thailand's most captivating festivals, it's held to honour the spirits of the water at a time when all the fields are flooded and the canals and rivers are bursting their banks. Sukhothai Historical Park, with its thirteenth-century temple ruins, is one of the most popular places to watch the festivities: for several nights around the full moon its ruins are wreathed in lights and its ponds shimmer in the reflected light of thousands of candles.

15.876842, -90.147114

**CANDELARIA,
GUATEMALA**

The limestone mountains of Alta Verapaz are riddled with
caves, of which the most impressive and extensive are
those at Candelaria, northeast of Chisec, where the river
has formed an astonishingly complex warren of caverns and
passages. The cave network extends for 22km – though if
you include all the subsidiary systems it's more like 80km
– and includes some truly monumental chambers. The
largest is the 200-metre-long, 60-metre-wide "Tzul Tacca",
where skylight shafts create a spectacular light-show on
the rocks and cavern water below. The cave was considered
by the ancient Maya to be the entrance to the underworld
of Xibalba; incense burners, smashed and burnt pots and
hundreds of obsidian blades found in the cave are evidence
of the age-old rituals that took place here.

14.356752, 100.568386

**AYUTTHAYA,
THAILAND**

In its heyday as the booming capital of the Thai kingdom, Ayutthaya, 80km north of Bangkok, was so well endowed with temples that sunlight reflecting off their gilt decoration was said to dazzle from 5km away. Today, wide, grassy spaces occupy much of the atmospheric site, which now resembles a graveyard for temples. The overgrown Wat Phra Mahathat – the epitome of Ayutthaya's nostalgic atmosphere of faded majesty – was built to house the remains of the Buddha himself: according to the royal chronicles, the fourteenth-century king Ramesuan was looking out of his palace one morning when ashes of the Buddha materialized out of thin air here. A gold casket containing the ashes was duly enshrined in a grand 38-metre-high prang. You can climb what remains of the prang to get a good view of the broad, grassy complex, with dozens of brick spires tilting at impossible angles and headless Buddhas scattered around like spare parts in a scrapyard – look out for the serene head of a stone Buddha that has become nestled in the embrace of a bodhi tree's roots.

19.314165, -155.060005

**HAWAII,
USA**

According to the classic popular image, a volcano is a cone-shaped mountain, with a neat round crater at the top that's filled with bubbling lava; Hawaiian volcanoes aren't like that. The island's shield volcanoes grow slowly and steadily rather than violently, adding layer upon layer as lava seeps out of fissures and vents all along the "rift zones" that cover their sides. The result is a long, low profile, supposedly resembling a warrior's shield laid on the ground. Walking across flaky, crumbling, new lava is an extraordinary experience. Every surface is like sandpaper, a fall can shred your skin and, even far from the apparent centre of activity, the ground can be too hot to touch. The sight of liquid rock oozing towards you, swirling with phlegmy gobbets and destroying all it touches; the crackle as it crunches across older layers of lava; the sudden flash as a dried-out tree bursts into flame: all leave you with a disconcerting sense of the land itself as a living, moving organism.

37.890184, -6.562958
**GRUTA DE LAS MARAVILLAS,
ANDALUCÍA, SPAIN**

After trudging round the sights of Seville in the furnace-like heat of high summer, taking a lungful of the refreshingly sharp and clear air of lofty Aracena, some 90km northwest, is something of a relief. Wilting sightseers can cool off further by entering the hollows of the Gruta de las Maravillas, Aracena's principal sight, and the largest and arguably the most impressive cave in Spain. Supposedly discovered by a local boy in search of a lost pig, the cave is now illuminated to allow visitors a peek at its astonishingly beautiful interior. Guided tours lead you through a series of chambers, the last of which may come as a surprise: it's known as the Sala de los Culos (Room of the Bottoms), its walls and ceiling an outrageous, naturally sculpted exhibition, tinged a pinkish orange in the light.

-18.863342, -69.133959

SALAR DE SURIRE, CHILE

Chile's formidable natural barriers – the immense Pacific, the lofty Andes and the desolate Atacama – have prevented contact between its animal species and their counterparts on the rest of the continent, resulting in an exceptional degree of endemism: one third of Chile's mammals are not found anywhere else in the world. The country's birdlife is dazzlingly varied, too, and even experienced ornithologists will swoon at Chile's many endemics and oddities, from tiny hummingbirds to giant condors, via raucous parrots, comical penguins and pink flamingoes. High in the Andes near the Bolivian border, several species of the latter gather at remote saltwater lakes, including the James's flamingo, which was thought to be extinct for fifty years until its rediscovery in the 1950s. The most magnificently hued of the flamingoes, it has a delicate pinkish tinge, bursting into a crimson at the base of the neck that gradually fades over the wings.

13.187099, -59.580016
**WELCHMAN HALL GULLY,
BARBADOS**

The dramatic Welchman Hall Gully in central Barbados is a long, deep corridor of jungle, hemmed in by steep cliffs and abounding with local flora and fauna. Though created aeons ago by a fissure in the limestone cap that covers this part of Barbados, the gully is named after a Welshman, General Williams, an early settler on the island and the first owner of the surrounding land. A handful of non-indigenous plants have been planted here over the years, but the vegetation is not dissimilar to that which covered the whole island when the British first arrived: prolific fruit and spice trees – nutmeg, clove and fig – dangling with lianas provide welcome shade, and numerous ginger lilies, ferns and palms offer a unique glimpse of the island in its primal state. Keep an eye out for the green monkeys, which can be spotted playing around in the undergrowth in the early morning or late afternoon. First brought to Barbados from West Africa around 1650 as pets of the slave traders, troupes of these mischievous creatures still lope around the island's interior.

40.518990, -108.988023
COLORADO,
USA

Colorado's northwest corner remains one of the state's least-visited regions – so far off the beaten track that Butch Cassidy and the Wild Bunch considered it a remote enough place to hole up in. Though it was commonly known that the area once teemed with a miscellany of dinosaurs, it wasn't until the 1909 discovery of eight brontosaurus tailbones that the rush to excavate really started. The supremely photogenic Dinosaur National Monument was originally created to preserve the precious paleontological remains embedded in its vast bulk; eventually, park boundaries were extended upstream along the picturesque Yampa and Green River canyons to include a swathe of rugged badlands, in which a maze of gorges harbour some stunning Native American rock art sites.

52.765472, 5.117974

**IJSSELMEER,
THE NETHERLANDS**

As your plane comes in to land at Amsterdam's Schiphol Airport it's worth remembering that two hundred years ago, the runway would have been under a lake. Huge tracts of the Netherlands have been reclaimed from the sea – like much of the country, the IJsselmeer, a shallow lake that was formerly sea, would be flooded without its dyke. Everywhere you look, the Netherlands' landscapes are defined by this fact: its chequered farmland, divided by drainage ditches; the windmills that still speckle the skyline; and of course the canals that skewer the centres of most Dutch towns. It's testament to the ingenuity of the Dutch that they have turned these measures to their advantage: at the same time as ensuring the safety of their people, they've created vital new land in what is one of the most congested countries in the world.

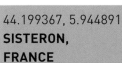

44.199367, 5.944891
SISTERON,
FRANCE

The first sight of Sisteron reveals its strategic significance as the major mountain gateway of Provence, with its citadel standing as a fearsome sentinel over the city and the solitary bridge across the river. During his famous return from exile in 1815, on his journey to overthrow Louis XVIII, Napoleon decided to cross the Alps, taking the most isolated snowbound mule paths up to Sisteron, to avoid the Rhône Valley and the troops in Marseilles. But the town gave Napoleon something of a headache: its mayor and most of its population were royalist, and given the fortifications and geography of the town, it was impossible for him to pass undetected. However, luck was still with Napoleon in those days, as the regional military commander was a sympathizer and removed all ammunition from Sisteron's arsenal. Napoleon is said to have sat nonchalantly on the bridge, contemplating the citadel above and the tumultuous waters below, while the town's notables, ordered to keep their pistols under wraps, looked on impotently. Eventually Napoleon entered the city, stopping off at a tavern for lunch before taking leave of Provence.

34.903960, -115.725174

**THE MOJAVE DESERT,
CALIFORNIA, USA**

Desolate, silent and virtually lifeless, the Mojave Desert, mythic badland of the West, has no equal when it comes to hardship. Apart from the huge dust-covered trucks that trundle across the state to Nevada and beyond, your only company here is likely to be hardcore bikers and neo-hippies: as the backdrop for a legion of road movies spawned by the underground film culture in the late 1960s and early 1970s, the Mojave's barren panorama has cult appeal. The immense Mojave National Preserve makes an ideal spot to take a break from the freeway and maybe camp out a night or two to prepare for the excesses of nearby Las Vegas. Scrambling around the spectacular Kelso Dunes, a golden 8km stretch reaching as high as 200m, is fun but disorientating: with nothing man-made to compare them to, these vast mountains of sand can certainly skew your sense of perspective.

-43.443413, 170.172815

**WESTLAND NATIONAL PARK,
SOUTH ISLAND, NEW ZEALAND**

Around 150km south of Hokitika on New Zealand's West Coast, two gleaming white rivers of ice force their way down towards the thick rainforest of the coastal plain, forming a palpable connection between the coast and the highest alpine peaks. As legend has it, a beautiful Maori girl named Hinehukatere loved walking in the mountains so much that she encouraged her lover, Tawe, to climb alongside her. He slipped and fell to his death, and Hinehukatere cried so copiously that her tears formed glaciers, known to Maori as Ka Riomata o Hinehukatere – "The Tears of the Avalanche Girl". Now going by the somewhat less poetic monikers of Franz Josef and Fox, these are two of the largest and most impressive of the sixty-odd glaciers that creak off the South Island's icy backbone, together forming the centrepiece of the rugged Westland National Park.

People

The journey from Gabes to Matmata in a rickety old louage should have been half an hour of chilling out to Tunisian radio while playing "Spot the Jedi Knight" through the window. In the event, I was unlucky enough to have a driver who imagined himself a champion of Formula One. Two hours, a high-speed blowout and several thousand olive trees later, I was rewarded with the sight of mystical Matmata with its vast, undulating landscapes and pit dwellings, home to the very independent Berbers. Well worth the bumpy ride.

Roger d'Olivere Mapp, *Photographer for The Rough Guide to Tunisia*

33.542713, 9.967464
**MATMATA,
TUNISIA**

Matmata's international fame derives almost exclusively from the original *Star Wars* film (or *Episode IV: A New Hope*, as it's known to die-hard fans). George Lucas and his crew set up stage in this tiny town in 1976, lured by its otherworldly troglodyte homes, cave-like dwellings dug out of soft sandstone. Unexpectedly, the futuristic film ended up taking many of its cues from the traditional Berber community: the subterranean Hotel Sidi Driss posed as Luke Skywalker's home, the nearby saltpans were the backdrop for Dune Sea and local clothing served as costume inspiration. The existence of the Matmata Berbers had only really come to light a few years earlier, when floods inundated their underground homes in the 1960s. From the Romans right up to the twentieth century, waves of foreign invaders had targeted the coast, 50km away, leaving Matmata's Berbers, and their age-old culture and traditions, largely undisturbed.

52.364797, 4.882398

**AMSTERDAM,
THE NETHERLANDS**

Sex clubs, gay clubs, tourist hubs and superclubs – Amsterdam nightlife is many things to many people, a wonderfully eclectic mix that both meets and surpasses visitors' expectations of sex, drugs and hard-house. As in London or New York, Amsterdam's superclubs pull in the young, the beautiful and the cutting edge, but the key difference is the freewheeling Dutch attitude of inclusion. Nowhere is this more apparent than at the annual Queen's Day celebrations at the end of April, one of the hottest events on the club calendar, when the street party spills over into two nights of flamboyant debauchery that rivals anything Rio has to offer. Shake off your preconceptions, don an orange wig, and you'll soon be welcomed into the fray as an honourary Amsterdammer.

-13.319496, -71.596699

PAUCARTAMBO, PERU

Despite the sometimes hectic pace that permeates Peru's capital, Lima, the prevailing attitude among most Peruvians is that there's always enough time for life's small pleasures: a chat, a ceviche or a good knees-up. Any excuse will do, but most celebrations are rooted in the country's ethnic traditions. Visit the pretty village of Paucartambo, in southern Peru, in mid-July and you're likely to be swept up in a huge mass of frenzied, costumed dancers, celebrating the Fiesta de la Virgen del Carmen – the culmination of six months of planning. Locals don grotesque blue-eyed masks, long beards and outlandish costumes to act out a parody of the white man's powers – malaria, a post-Conquest problem, tends to be a central theme – in which an old man suffers terrible agonies until a Western medic appears on the scene, with the inevitable hypodermic in his hand. If he manages to save the old man (a rare occurrence) it's usually due to a dramatic muddling of prescriptions by his dancing assistants – and thus does Andean fate triumph over science.

-22.965011, -43.172305
RIO DE JANEIRO, BRAZIL

From the families that descend on Copacabana every Sunday to the muscle-bound hunks and bikini-clad lovelies of Ipanema, Rio's beaches shape the social life of all the city's inhabitants. These world-famous stretches of sand may attract hordes of tourists, but they're first and foremost the preserve of Cariocas, Rio's residents, many of whom treat their body as a project – to be nipped, tucked, built up, flexed, tanned and then flaunted. Plastic surgery is big business here: for a silicone-enhanced *bumbum turbinado, a lipo enzimática*, or for the downright vain, calf-muscle implants, Rio's Zona Sul is the centre of the industry. Those that shun the easy route to the body beautiful practise any number of beach sports – football, volleyball and *futevolei* – a look-no-hands combination of the two. Whether it's for their lack of footballing prowess or the modesty of their swimwear, most gringos stand out on Rio's beaches – but while Cariocas revel in looking good, there's no hint of condescension towards those less blessed.

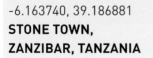-6.163740, 39.186881

**STONE TOWN,
ZANZIBAR, TANZANIA**

Stone Town's gruesome history as a centre of the slave trade is perhaps best understood by visiting Tippu Tip's House along the poetically named Suicide Alley. In the latter half of the nineteenth century, Tippu Tip was the richest and most powerful slave-trader in East Africa. Many a European explorer curried his favour to obtain safe passage on the mainland, as his influence – and fear of his name – spread along the caravan routes into eastern Congo. Although Tippu Tip's once opulent home is now in an advanced state of decay, its elaborate door and black-and-white marble steps still set it apart. The house is currently occupied by various local families, evidently undaunted by the popular belief that the house is haunted by the spirits of slaves.

13.917222, -61.046863
ST LUCIA

A fusion of French, British and African traditions, St Lucia's Creole culture is an intriguing mix. Though Christian hymns are sung lustily enough to raise the church roofs each Sunday, this is also a society in which esoteric African traditions of magic and spiritualism survive. Obeah, a secretive, mystical practice that also has its roots in African ancestor worship, is woven into the fabric of local life, despite the fact that it's ostensibly illegal. The more superstitious still call upon the obeahman to fix bad business partnerships and love gone awry, or to attempt the removal of jumbies, bad-tempered spirits that vex the life of the common man. The obeahman does his work through ritualistic use of herbs, rums, tobacco, potions and archaic incantations, but as anti-obeah laws are still occasionally enforced, it remains an arcane practice.

39.418533, -0.791327

**BUÑOL,
SPAIN**

La Tomatina – the tomato-throwing festival of Buñol – is about as wild and excessive as Spanish fiestas get. One day in late August, 30,000 people descend on a small provincial town, at the same time as a fleet of municipal trucks, carrying 120,000 tonnes of tomatoes. Tension builds. "To-ma-te, to-ma-te" yell the crowds. And then the truckers let them have it, hurling the ripe, pulpy fruit at everyone present. And everyone goes crazy, hurling the pulp back at the trucks, at each other, in the air…for an hour. At 1pm, an explosion signals the end of the battle and the local fire brigade arrives to hose down the combatants, buildings and streets. And then, miraculously, within the hour, everyone arrives back on the street, perfectly turned out, to enjoy the rest of the fiesta, which, oddly enough, includes such refined pursuits as orchestral concerts in the town's open-air auditorium.

-34.579050, -58.421044
**BUENOS AIRES,
ARGENTINA**

The gaucho who once roamed the pampas on horseback, knife clenched between teeth, leaving a trail of broken hearts and gnawed steak bones behind him, is as important a part of the collective romantic imagination as the Wild West cowboy is in the US. He emerged as a distinct figure in the nineteenth century, with roots in indigenous and Spanish culture and an evolution suited to the specific conditions of the pampas: the gaucho was totally self-sufficient, highly skilled on horseback and devilishly fast with that knife. Despised by both the rural landowning elite and the urban intelligentsia as barbaric and dangerous, gauchos lived outside society's strictures, moving wherever they could find work. It's estimated that they numbered 80,000 at their peak in the 1870s, but large-scale immigration, urbanization and technological progress sounded the death knell for the gaucho not long after. The freedoms represented by the lifestyle came to embody a sense of what it was to be a true Argentine – scratch the surface of most Porteños, and you'll find the proud and indomitable spirit of the gauchos, never more at home than when warming their feet by the fire and sharing a *mate*.

39.903333, 116.382873
**BEIJING,
CHINA**

Beijing opera (*jingxi*) is the most celebrated of China's 350 or so regional operatic styles – a unique combination of song, dance, acrobatics and mime. Most of the plots are based on historical or mythological themes, and are full of moral lessons; an interesting, if controversial, variation is opera dealing with contemporary themes, such as the struggle of women to marry as they choose. Highly stylized, to the outsider the performances can often seem obscure and wearying, as they're punctuated by a succession of crashing gongs and piercing, discordant singing. But it's worth seeing once, especially if you can acquaint yourself with the story beforehand. Even if you struggle to understand, the colours used on stage, from the costumes to the make-up on the players' faces, are helpfully symbolic: red signifies loyalty; yellow, fierceness; blue, cruelty; and white, evil.

43.842458, 10.502163

**LUCCA,
ITALY**

Italians are fashionistas to the tips of their manicured fingernails. The northern city of Milan is the style capital of the country; the city's Quadrilatero d'Oro (Gold Quarter) is packed with eye-wateringly expensive designer stores, while Milan Fashion Week is one of the major staging posts in the fashion-pack calendar. But unabashed Milanese style – gilt-laden, glitzy, and enveloped in fur in winter – is a little hard-edged for most tastes. Elsewhere in the country you'll see a less effortful approach to the characteristically Italian concept of "fare bella figura", which, put simply, means looking good and feeling good, even when you're putting out the rubbish or sitting on a street corner having an ice cream (and the phrase applies as much to the country's well-groomed men as to the women). In the elegant Tuscan city of Lucca, a slim-fitting scarlet ensemble and a medieval backdrop transform the simple passeggiata – the customary evening promenade – into an all-Italian catwalk moment.

38.908759, 1.437243
**IBIZA TOWN,
IBIZA, SPAIN**

Ibiza's clubbing scene is ludicrously out of proportion to its modest population and in high season the superclubs have bloated capacities that need filling every day of the week. One of the strategies used by club promoters to publicize their nights are club parades: processions of costumed dancers bearing banners that weave through the labyrinthine lanes of the port area in Ibiza Town. Gay nights tend to go for über-ripped pec-baring gym junkies, or use a theatrical theme like the Moulin Rouge, sending out cancan dancers who high-kick their way from bar to bar. It's customary for bar owners to give out free *chupitos* (liquor shots) to all in these parades, so there are some seriously sozzled participants by the end of their grand tour around the lanes. Parades terminate in Carrer d'Alfons XII, under the shadow of Ibiza's mighty medieval walls. By 1am, this small plaza is rammed with all manner of extrovert humanity, with an excess of drag queens, exposed flesh and exhibitionists and fetishists of every sexual and satirical persuasion.

15.406488, -91.145555

NEBAJ, GUATEMALA

Although the Maya people may appear quiet and humble, their costumes, fiestas and markets are a riot of colour, creativity and celebration. Most Maya are extremely attached to local values and traditions – not least their eye-catching costumes – and regard themselves as *indígenas* first and Guatemalans second. One of the best opportunities to see Maya traditions at close quarters is at the weekly market, when highland villages are filled by a steady flow of people, arriving by pick-up or bus, on foot or by donkey. The plaza buzzes with activity, although raised voices are a rarity, with deals struck after protracted, but always polite, negotiations. Perhaps the most enjoyable of Guatemala's markets are in tiny, isolated hamlets: up high in the folds of the mountains, traders and villagers barter and banter in near-whispers and the hushed clicks of the local dialect, in the unhurried ritual that so defines Maya highland life.

31.220926, -7.671279

SETTI FATMA, ATLAS MOUNTAINS, MOROCCO

You don't have to be a snake to be charmed in Morocco. Having boarded your twenty-first-century metal magic carpet, you disembark in a land of the *djinns* (spirits), steeped in the intensity and exoticism of Africa. And nothing maintains the illusion that by travelling a couple of hours forward you've gone a century or two back like Morocco's street entertainers. Here, public squares are miniature carnivals where acrobats from Tazeroualt cartwheel, storytellers narrate within circles of listeners and Gnaoua musicians trance out to repetitive drums and cymbals like ancient techno. You'll also stroll past monkey trainers, henna painters and astrologers, or Berber doctors who sit patiently with their cures – dessicated lizards and ostrich eggs, feathers and dried herbs. And, of course, there are the snake charmers, who pipe nasal, oboe-like *ghaitahs* at swaying cobras or puff adders. Take a photo and you'll be expected to hand over a few dirhams – indeed, many traders rely on tourists for survival. Yet this is not all fodder for foreigners: much of it is as authentic as it is exotic. Once bitten, you'll find Morocco stays in your blood.

27.671979, 85.427118

**BAKTAPUR,
NEPAL**

The number of travellers who return from Nepal and say that, for all the breathtaking scenery, it was the people they liked the most, is astonishing. Nepali friendliness is proverbial, yet neither the shared traits of this tough, proud people nor Nepal's modest size should obscure the variety of its inhabitants. The country has a continent's share of ethnic groups, with more than fifty languages and as many cultural traditions. The Kathmandu Valley has its own indigenous group: the Newars, whose tight-knit communities are recognizable by their distinctive architecture of warm brick and carved wood. The Newars could be said to represent a mix of all Nepal's cultures: they are Hindus and Buddhists at the same time; they look by turns "Indian" and "Tibetan". But it would be more true to say that they represent the culture which is Nepal – including that of extraordinary religious and ethnic tolerance, which persists, admirably, today.

36.777122, -6.355478
SANLÚCAR DE BARRAMEDA, SPAIN

Although there's been a settlement at Sanlúcar de Barrameda, on Spain's Cádiz coast, since Roman times, it wasn't until the recapture of the town in 1264 by Alfonso X that it grew to become one of sixteenth-century Spain's leading ports. Columbus sailed from here on his third voyage to the Americas and it was also from here in 1519 that Magellan set out to circumnavigate the globe. Today, Sanlúcar's maritime pedigree is celebrated in the curious Museo del Mar Caracoles, a bizarre lifetime collection of objects retrieved from the sea by eccentric proprietor Garrido García. Something of a latter-day Long John Silver, Señor García proudly conducts tours around his house/museum — a treasure trove of maritime knick-knacks — with a feral pigeon perched on one shoulder.

28.380074, 83.811178
**GHANDRUK,
NEPAL**

Nepal's western hills are the country at its most scenic, with roaring gorges, precariously perched villages and terraced fields reaching to improbable heights, and some of the most graceful and accessible peaks of the Himalayas for a backdrop. Yet in this, Nepal's most populous hill region, the people are the dominant feature of the landscape. Magars and Gurungs, the most visible ethnic groups here, enjoy an earthily traditional, but relatively prosperous, existence: houses are tidy and spacious, and hill women festoon themselves with the family gold. The prosperity comes, indirectly, from an unlikely quarter: the western hills were historically the most important recruiting area for Gurkha soldiers, long rated among the finest fighting units in the world.

10.085358, 77.057719
**KERALA,
INDIA**

One of India's smallest but most remarkable states, Kerala is quite unlike anywhere else in the subcontinent. Not just a place of supreme natural beauty, from the idyllic palm-fringed beaches and lagoons of the coast to the breezy inland hills, it's also a culturally vibrant place with no end of fascinating traditions and festivals. More than anything, though, Kerala serves as a notable success story in a nation still racked with poverty and ethnic turbulence, with life expectancy and living standards well above the national average, a literacy rate of around 90 percent, and an unusually diverse and peaceable array of religious and political traditions. As such, the state provides a beacon of optimism in the often troubled fabric of present-day India and, with its fusion of traditional culture and forward-looking contemporary nous, serves as an inspiring example of what the entire country may one day eventually become.

Structures

I was behind schedule, but I'd heard San Luis was amazing and I couldn't resist investigating. Stepping through the doorway, I was speechless: every conceivable space was decorated with Baroque Gothic plasterwork. The church was empty with the exception of its keeper, a lone figure on a wooden chair, whose cassette player was blaring Bach at full volume. The only way to take a picture of the central dome without distorting perspective was to lie flat on my back, much to the surprise of the caretaker. San Luis represents what I love about travel photography: the surprises, and how you come across them.

Georgie Scott, *Photographer for The Rough Guide to Andalucía*

37.39834, -5.988316
SAN LUIS DE LOS FRANCESES, SEVILLE, SPAIN

Think of Seville and you'll probably picture the Giralda, your mind's eye conjuring up an image of the beautifully crafted minaret that towers over the city's central plaza. Certainly, you'll picture the cathedral, the largest Gothic church in the world and an architectural celebration of the return of Christian rule to southern Spain. What you won't imagine is the Iglesia de San Luis de los Franceses, ushered away, with minimum fuss, to the working-class quarter of La Macarena to the west. Seemingly lost to much of the outside world, this quiet Jesuit church is one of the finest examples of Baroque architecture in Europe, its flamboyant facade made all the more grandiose by its unexpected appearance, squeezed between narrow houses down a tidy little backstreet. Built at the turn of the eighteenth century, the church is designed in the shape of a Greek cross; inside, the striking altarpieces and delicate murals stretch skywards to the magnificent dome, shafts of sunlight bathing the interior in an ethereal white.

43.947264, 4.535326
**PONT DU GARD,
FRANCE**

The Pont du Gard is the greatest surviving stretch of a 50km-long Roman aqueduct built in the middle of the first century AD to supply fresh water to Nîmes. With just a seventeen-metre difference in altitude between start and finish, the aqueduct was quite an achievement, running as it does over hill and dale, through a tunnel, along the top of a wall, into trenches and over rivers. Three tiers of arches span the River Gardon, with the covered water conduit rendered with a special plaster and waterproofed with a paint thought to be based on fig juice. Today, the bridge is a UNESCO World Heritage Site and something of a tourist trap, but is nonetheless a supreme combination of function and aesthetics. The best way to get up close and personal to this architectural marvel is to follow the hundreds of French visitors who descend on a sunny day: make for the rocky banks of the river, don your swimming gear and take to the water. Propelled by the gentle current of the reassuringly shallow Gard, you can float right under the arch, which casts a dense shadow onto the turquoise water.

-34.609477, -58.385811

**BUENOS AIRES,
ARGENTINA**

Avenida de Mayo's most striking building, the Edificio Barolo, is a weird but handsome blend of Neo-Romanesque, Neo-Gothic and Indian temple. Designed by Italian architect Mario Palanti and constructed between 1919 and 1923, it was created as a monument to Dante's *Divine Comedy*, and is full of references to the epic poem – its three sections represent Hell, Purgatory and Heaven, its height in metres equals the number of songs (100) and it has 22 floors, the same as the number of stanzas in each canto. Moreover, in early June, the roof's tip aligns with the Southern Cross constellation – the "entrance to heaven". Tours of the building explain its symbolism, all the way from the imposing lobby to the glass dome and lighthouse way up at the giddying tip.

21.878195, -82.766705
ISLA DE LA JUVENTUD, CUBA

Built in 1926 by its future inmates, Cuba's "Model Prison" was at the time considered the definitive example of efficient design, as up to six thousand prisoners – including one-time inmate Fidel Castro – could be controlled with a minimum of staff. Every moment of the prisoners' lives was on view through the iron bars, and the gun slits cut into the grim tower in the dead centre of each block allowed one guard and his rifle to control nearly a thousand inmates from a position of total safety. The prison soon became infamous for unprecedented levels of corruption and cruelty, however, and the last prisoner was released in 1967. Now unmanned and falling into disrepair, the four huge cylindrical cell blocks still feel as oppressive as they must have been when crammed with inmates.

36.113261, -115.176651
CHANDELIER, BELLAGIO HOTEL, LAS VEGAS, USA

Las Vegas' fabled Strip started out as the main desert highway into town from California; everyone drove, and nobody walked. The earliest casino-hotels stood set back in majesty, with room to park on every side. Lured in by giant neon signs, vehicles would sweep up their grand driveways, to be greeted by valets beneath elaborate porte-cochères. Once inside, you were all but trapped; even if you could find an exit, the nearest neighbour might be half a mile away, and there wasn't even a sidewalk. As more casinos sprang up, and the traffic slowed to a crawl, pedestrians began to venture outside. The casinos built over their parking lots, replacing them with eye-catching spectaculars – a volcano spouting real fire here, a soaring Eiffel Tower there. Now there's almost no space left; strolling the Strip, you step from ancient Rome to Paris to Renaissance Venice in a matter of moments. Each casino merges into the next, and architectural theorists can't decide what to call them any more. If a casino facade consists of live actors crewing two battling pirate ships, then is it even a building?

-34.581798, -58.393965

**BUENOS AIRES,
ARGENTINA**

Among the attractions of Recoleta, Buenos Aires' grandest barrio, is the startling Floralis Genérica, a 25-metre aluminium and stainless steel metallic flower that opens and shuts. One of the city's newest sculptures, it was donated in April 2002 by Argentine architect Eduardo Catalano as a tribute to all the world's flowers and, in his words, a symbol of "hope for the country's new spring" – a reference to the 2001 crisis, which saw widespread rioting in the capital. A system of light sensors and hydraulics closes the six petals at sunset and opens them again at 8am – the sculptor was afraid people would miss it if it opened at daybreak – but they stay open all night long on May 25, September 21 (the beginning of spring), Christmas Eve and New Year's Eve.

41.008539, 28.977867
ISTANBUL,
TURKEY

The Yerebatan Sarnıçı or "Sunken Cistern" is one of several such underground structures in Istanbul, and the first to have been extensively excavated. Probably built in the fourth century, and enlarged in the sixth, this cavernous space was supplied by aqueducts with water from the Belgrade Forest. The cistern fell into disuse after the Ottoman conquest and its existence was only brought to public attention in 1545 by the Frenchman Petrus Gyllius, who was led here by locals who had sunk wells into the cistern. They even kept boats on the water from which they could fish its depths – Gyllius' interest was first aroused when he found fresh fish being sold in the streets nearby. In 1987, fifty thousand tons of mud and water were removed, and the walls and columns fortified. James Bond had to row his way through the forest of columns in *From Russia With Love*, but these days raised pathways make exploration of the site easier. Despite the piped muzak, the cistern is deeply atmospheric, with carp swimming lazily through the floodlit waters and water dripping steadily from the vaults above.

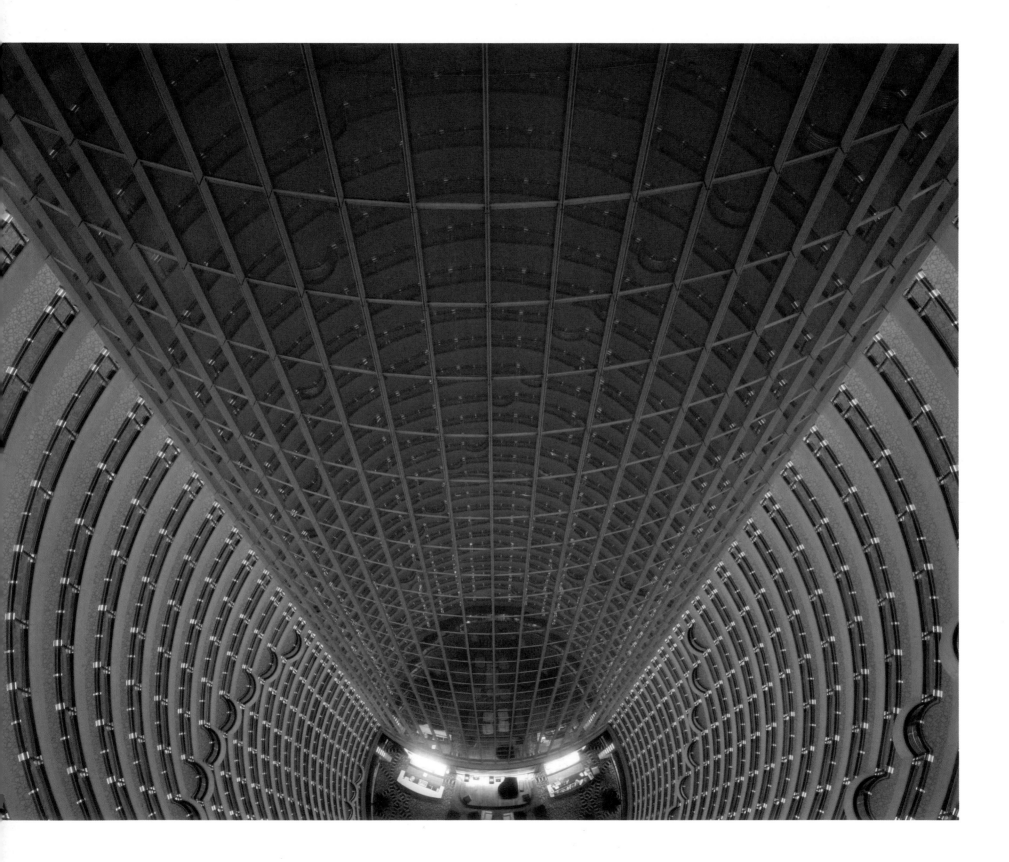

Shanghai's most striking modern building, the Jinmao Tower is an elegantly tapering postmodern take on Art Deco. All the proportions are based on the lucky number eight – the 88 floors are divided into sixteen segments, each of which is one-eighth shorter than the sixteen-storey base – but never mind the mathematics, the harmony is obvious at first glance. What looks from a distance like filigree are actually decorative metal struts, which make the building appear eminently possible to climb; indeed, in 2001 it was scaled, apparently on a whim, by a visiting shoe salesman. The most recent adventurer to ignore the "no climbing" signs around the base was urban climber Alain "Spiderman" Robert in 2007, who climbed to the top and back in ninety minutes without harnesses or ropes – and was promptly arrested. An ear-popping lift whisks you up 340m to the top in a matter of seconds, where the observation deck offers sublime views of the city. It's quite a sight, but before making your descent, turn around: the giddying view back down the building's glorious galleried atrium is not to be missed.

While travellers from all over the globe converge on Machu Picchu and the well-trodden Inca Trail in southern Peru, the less-visited Sacred Valley, to the east, is also endowed with sites of jaw-dropping splendour. Of all the ancient ruins within reach of the vibrant, colourful city of Cusco, known to the Incas as the "navel of the world", perhaps none are more spectacular than the Inca site of Moray. Part agricultural centre and part ceremonial, the ruins are deep, bowl-like depressions in the earth, the largest about 30m deep and comprising seven concentric circular stone terraces, facing inward and diminishing in radius like a multi-layered roulette wheel. Such is the depth of the pits that the temperature can vary by as much as 15° C between the top and the bottom.

8.348645, 80.397263
**ANURADHAPURA,
SRI LANKA**

The pure white dome of the Buddhist stupa – or dagoba, as they're called in Sri Lanka – is one of the island's most characteristic sights, and you won't travel far without passing one of these elegant edifices rising up out of the palm trees or paddy fields. As popular legend has it, the dagoba's distinctive form can be traced back to the Buddha himself: upon being asked by his followers what shape a memorial to him should take, he is said to have folded his robe into a square and placed his upturned begging bowl and umbrella on top of it. There are six different varieties (from the stumpy "heap of rice paddy" shape to the elongated "bell" shape), and the exterior designs run the gamut from severely plain to ornate examples decorated with stylized bo tree leaves and vines. They also come in many different sizes; the three great dagobas of Anuradhapura, amongst the largest man-made structures of the ancient world, are Asia's nearest equivalent to the Egyptian pyramids. The foundations were trampled down by elephants, then the main body of the dagobas filled with rubble and vast quantities of bricks – it's been estimated that the Jetavana dagoba at Anuradhapura uses almost one hundred million.

42.361647, -71.091628
**CAMBRIDGE,
USA**

Despite looking like a set of egg timers designed by Salvador Dalí, the Stata Center in Cambridge, Massachusetts, is the $200-million work of renowned architect Frank Gehry. An appropriately off-the-wall design for Boston's laid-back, arty sister city, the building was opened in 2004 to house the Computer, Information and Intelligence Science's departments of the Massachusetts Institute of Technology, in a project partly funded by Bill Gates of Microsoft. The interior is no less intriguing: walls lean at dizzying angles, materials clash and the views from the tilting windows have been known to induce vertigo. The whole is intended to be a metaphor for the minds of the researchers within: creative, innovative – and far from square.

30.322960, 35.449587

**PETRA,
JORDAN**

Ever since a western adventurer stumbled on the site of Petra in 1812, it has fired imaginations, its grandeur and dramatic setting pushing it – like the Pyramids and the Taj Mahal – into the realms of legend. In its Nabatean golden age, Petra was an extravagantly wealthy city, home to tens of thousands of people. Temples and public buildings were built on a grand scale, watercourses flowed to irrigate lush gardens and the natural earth tones of the buildings were tempered by brightly coloured plasterwork. Though many of Petra's grand buildings are now rubbly excavation sites, there's still plenty here to take your breath away – not least the awe-inspiring Monastery. With a facade of almost fifty square metres – the doorway alone is taller than a house – it almost seems like an optical illusion.

33.845466, -117.997928
**LOS ANGELES,
USA**

It's hard to escape the clutches of Disneyland, even when you leave: everything in the surrounding area is built around it, from diners to dive bars. But the thrill rides at Knott's Berry Farm, 6km northwest, go some way to restoring antique notions of what amusement parks used to be like. The park was born during the Depression when people began lining up for the fried-chicken dinners prepared by Mrs Knott, a local farmer's wife. To amuse the children while they waited for their food, Mr Knott reconstructed a Wild West ghost town and added amusements, until the park had grown into the sprawling site you see today. These days, it's all about the roller coasters: Montezooma's Revenge is the original one-loop coaster; the forwards-and-backwards Boomerang can easily induce nausea; Supreme Scream is a delightfully terrifying freefall nose-dive; and the Perilous Plunge is a hellish drop at a 75-degree angle – far more exciting than any old log-flume ride.

-22.907919, -43.125908
NITERÓI,
BRAZIL

Cariocas have a tendency to sneer at Niterói, typically commenting that the only good thing about the city is its views back across Guanabara Bay to Rio. It's certainly true that the vistas are absolutely breathtaking on a clear day, but Niterói has much more to offer, not least for admirers of the work of the celebrated Brazilian architect Oscar Niemeyer. Located just south of the centre on a promontory, the Niemeyer-designed Museu de Arte Contemporânea offers a 360-degree perspective of Niterói and across the bay to Rio, and even Niemeyer's hardened critics find it difficult to find fault with the building's spectacular flying-saucer-shaped curves.

48.858798, 2.294362

PARIS,
FRANCE

Standing sentinel over a great bend in the Seine, the
monumental flagpole that is the Eiffel Tower remains
an endlessly inspirational sight, however tired of mega-
monuments you may be. It's hard to believe that the
quintessential symbol both of Paris and the brilliance of
industrial engineering was designed to be a temporary
structure for a fair. Late nineteenth-century Europe had a
taste for giant-scale, colonialist–capitalist extravaganzas,
but Paris's 1889 Exposition Universelle was particularly
ambitious: when completed, the tower, at 300m, was
the tallest building in the world. This most celebrated of
landmarks was only saved from demolition by the sudden
need for "wireless telegraphy" aerials in the first decade of
the twentieth century. The tower's role in telecommunications
– its only function apart from tourism – has only become
more important, and the original crown is now masked by an
efflorescence of antennae. Outside daylight hours, distinctive
sodium lights illuminate the structure, and a double
searchlight was added for the millennium celebrations,
making its first sweep at midnight on December 31. For the
first ten minutes of every hour, thousands of effervescent
lights now scramble and fizz about the structure, defining the
famous silhouette in luminescent champagne.

39.504323, 2.520912
**MAGALUF,
MALLORCA**

To the surprise of many first-time visitors, for the most part Mallorca remains a beautiful and frequently fascinating place, from the craggy mountains of its north coast through to the old towns of the central plain. The island's sometimes negative image was spawned by the helter-skelter development of the 1960s, which transformed tracts of the coastline into bargain-basement resort towns such as Magaluf. The town finally lost patience with its youthful British visitors in 1996, when the local authorities won a court order allowing them to demolish twenty downmarket hotels in an attempt to end – or at least control – the debauchery that had come to characterize the resort. The high-rise hotels were duly dynamited and an extensive clean-up programme freshened up Magaluf's appearance. These extreme measures have brought some improvement, but the resort's British visitors remain steadfastly determined to create, or at least patronize, a bizarre caricature of their homeland: it's all here, from beans-on-toast with Marmite to lukewarm pints of lager.

-15.819404, -69.970958
**TITICACA,
PERU**

The man-made Uros Floating Islands, adrift in serene Lake Titicaca, are weird to walk over and even stranger to live on. Inhabited since their construction centuries ago by Uros Indians retreating from more powerful neighbours like the Incas, the islands last around twelve to fifteen years and it takes two months of communal work to create a new one. Layer upon layer of totora reeds, the dominant plant in the shallows of Titicaca, form the basic construction, as well as being a source of food – the inner juicy bits near the roots – and material for roofing, walling and fishing rafts. Life on the islands is certainly never easy: the inhabitants have to go some distance to find fresh water, and the undersides of the structures rot so rapidly that fresh matting has to be added constantly.

44.495218, 11.347997
**BOLOGNA,
ITALY**

One of Italy's best-looking cities, Bologna's centre is startlingly medieval in plan, a jumble of red brick, tiled roofs and balconies radiating out from the great central square of Piazza Maggiore. The most conspicuous remnants of Bologna's medieval layout are the Due Torri, the city's own "leaning towers" – rare survivors of the hundred-odd towers that loomed over Bologna in the twelfth century. Nobody can say for sure why they were built, but the most likely explanation is that the city's warring wealthy families used them for defensive purposes and as emblems of prestige. Over the centuries, fires, wars, lightning bolts and town planners have all wreaked dramatic changes on the city's skyline, and fewer than twenty towers still stand today. The 97-metre Torre degli Asinelli is not just useful for orientation when one medieval alleyway looks much like another: you can also climb its 498 steps for magnificent views over Bologna's rooftops.

64.141689, -21.926887

**REYKJAVÍK,
ICELAND**

Iceland's largest church is the magnificent Hallgrímskirkja, whose neatly composed space-shuttle-like form dominates the Reykjavík skyline. Work began on the church immediately after World War II but was only completed a few years ago, the slow progress due to the task being carried out by a family firm — comprising one man and his son. The church's outlandish design — not least its 73-metre steeple — has divided the city over the years and the locals have grown to accept rather than love it. But the design does possess one feature which even its critics can't fault: the eighth-floor eyrie, which offers magnificent views over Reykjavík's rooftops.

41.898755, -87.622967

CHICAGO,
USA

In an architectural prize-fight between America's biggest cities, there's little question that Chicago would win by a knockout, thanks to the sheer volume and variety of its grand buildings. At 344m, the Hancock Center offers a jaw-dropping 360° panorama – a good vantage point from which to take in lofty landmarks such as the ancient-looking Water Tower and the sleekly futuristic IBM Building. The Hancock Center's 94th-floor observatory has an open-air viewing deck where winds can force the building to sway as much as ten inches from side to side, though you probably won't even notice, so staggering are the views – you'll see as far as Indiana, Michigan and Wisconsin on a clear day. Two floors up in the Signature Room bar, you can take in the same panorama in comfort for the price of a drink.

51.056346, 3.721876

**GHENT,
BELGIUM**

Ghent's beauty may be eclipsed by that of its ancient rival, Bruges, but it still musters some superb Gothic buildings and a bevy of delightful, intimate streetscapes, where its distinctive brick houses are woven around a skein of narrow canals. The atmosphere here is markedly different from that of its neighbour, however, and Ghent remains a quintessentially Flemish city, with the tourist industry supplementing, rather than dominating, the local economy. As a consequence, it preserves the raw and authentic edges that Bruges has tried so hard to iron out, and its busy centre reflects the city's ancient class and linguistic divide: the streets south of the Korenmarkt tend to be straight and wide, lined with elegant old mansions – the former habitations of the wealthier, French-speaking classes – while to the north, Flemish Ghent is all narrow alleys and low brick houses.

-42.484036, -73.76255

**CASTRO,
CHILE**

Built at the head of a twenty-kilometre fjord on Chiloé Island, Castro has had its fair share of difficulties: struck several times
by natural disasters since the first recorded earthquake in 1646, most of its old town has been burned, knocked down or
washed away over the years. A few days before the catastrophic 1936 fire that just about burned Castro to the ground, several
residents reported seeing a giant sea lion come out of the water and waddle up the street. In a community where superstition
is second nature, this apparition was widely accepted as an evil omen. Perhaps it was, though you didn't really need an omen to
foresee the danger: Castro of the 1930s was a fire waiting to happen, built as it was almost entirely of back-to-back wooden
buildings. When the fire struck, all the inhabitants could do was head for the sea, where they watched their homes burn from the
waters of the icy fjord. Miraculously, some buildings have survived the various disasters, such as the groups of brightly coloured
palafitos (houses on stilts) on the waterfront. The last remaining such structures in the country, the local government is torn
between preserving them as national monuments and condemning them as insanitary slums.

44.845364, -0.574797
**BORDEAUX,
FRANCE**

On Bordeaux's Esplanade des Quinconces, one of Europe's biggest squares, the Monument aux Girondins is a fittingly grandiose affair. This glorious *fin-de-siècle* ensemble of statues and fountains was built in honour of the influential local deputies to the 1789 Revolutionary Assembly, later purged by Robespierre as moderates and counter-revolutionaries. During World War II, in a fit of anti-French spite, the occupying Germans made plans to melt the monument down, only to be foiled by the local Resistance, who got there first and, under cover of darkness, dismantled it piece by piece and hid it in a barn in the Médoc for the duration of the war.

Time-wasting

I took this shot on my first ever commission for Rough Guides – ten days in Zanzibar can't be bad! Not everyone in the country is happy to be photographed so I asked a local to help me communicate and be as respectful of the culture as possible. I spotted this man on TV Corner – I liked the way he was sitting and was drawn to the colours of his shirt against the door. We asked his permission to take some photos and luckily he didn't move. Afterwards, we sat down and drank a coffee together.

Suzanne Porter, *Photographer for The Rough Guide to Zanzibar*

-6.16525, 39.191017
**STONE TOWN,
ZANZIBAR, TANZANIA**

Entertainment in Stone Town is appealingly low-key, epitomized by the old town's *barazas*, or benches, which have been a hub of community life for centuries. *Barazas* were built on each side of the town's long, narrow streets instead of pavements, and make a natural meeting point for all sections of society, who come here to gossip, play cards, sip a cup of piping arabica – the beans are roasted and ground on the smooth benches – or just laze away the afternoon. As night draws in, the entertainment is provided by the flickering screen of a communal TV. One of the liveliest *barazas* is in Sokomuhogo Square, whose popular name, Jaws Corner, derives from the film once shown on its resident television. Here and at nearby TV Corner, locals spend the evening glued to the screen, usually featuring pirated movies, more often than not bizarrely dubbed or subtitled into Chinese.

55.673463, 12.571090

**COPENHAGEN,
DENMARK**

Not many cities have a roller coaster, a pirate ship and an eighty-metre-high carousel slap-bang in their centre, but Copenhagen is home to Tivoli – probably the best fairground in the world. This famous pleasure garden has bewitched all comers since 1843, and to the Danes it's nothing short of a national treasure. Though there are few rides here to compete with the white-knuckle thrills of modern theme parks, the vast numbers of foreign visitors who flood through the gates each summer are drawn by the mix of old and new: rickety rides, old-world fairground stalls and charming landscaped gardens rub shoulders with head-spinning newcomers such as the Demon – a three-loop roller coaster. A few hours spent wandering among revellers of all ages indulging in the mass consumption of ice cream, with the squeals from the rides echoing round the park, is a memorable experience, while on a fine summer's night, with the twinkling illuminations and fireworks exploding overhead, it's nothing short of magical.

-34.569761, -58.398755

THE ROXIE, BUENOS AIRES, ARGENTINA

The Porteños – Buenos Aires' amenable residents – must rank as amongst the most laid-back on the planet. Take a seat at any of the city's cafés and you'll witness first-hand their talent for whiling away hours over a tiny cup of immaculate foamy espresso, in between reading, talking, gazing out of the window or stealing a kiss. The Roxie diner is on the Costanera, an embankment that runs alongside the Río de la Plata, perfect for a lazy afternoon stroll. But it's on balmy summer nights that this riverside strip comes alive, as fun-loving Porteños flock to its bars and clubs. When the rays of the dawn sun turn the river the glittering silver of its name, they're still here, chatting and sipping drinks, and in no particular hurry to head home – many clubs remain open until past midday. As any Porteño worthy of the name knows, that's when it's time for a siesta.

40.545304, 14.235521
**CAPRI,
ITALY**

No place is more glamorous than Capri, long the most sought-after destination in the Bay of Naples. This tiny isle of immense, weatherworn crags, jutting out of deep blue waters, was home to the mythical Sirens of the ancient world, and has been much eulogized as a playground of the super-rich ever since. But celebrity clientele notwithstanding, the island retains an unspoiled charm that's well worth seeking out, and it's still possible to have old-fashioned holiday fun here. The pebbly bucket-and-spade beach at Marina Piccola, with its shallow, calm lagoon, makes an appealingly low-key antidote to the glitz.

19.748892, 101.991320
**KOUANG SI WATERFALL,
LAOS**

One of the best day-trips from Louang Phabang, northern Laos, is to Kouang Si waterfall, a picturesque, multi-level affair that tumbles 60m before spilling through a series of crystal-blue pools. Head for the upper pool for lovely views of the falls, or if you feel like a swim, splash about in the lower pool. It's a great place for a picnic – and there are plenty of vendors nearby selling *tam màk hung* (spicy papaya salad) and cooling drinks. Once you've dipped your toes in, take the steep path on the opposite side of the falls, which leads to a grassy meadow filled with brilliantly coloured butterflies.

15.256980, 73.918977

**BENAULIM BEACH,
GOA**

Nod off for a second on any Goan beach and you can be sure your doze will be ruptured by the appearance of someone selling something, regardless of how much you appear to want it, or not: cheap cotton lunghis, baggy beach shorts, ice cream, slices of watermelon, jewellery, a massage and talking drums are just some of the goods on offer. But Goa's beaches offer stranger sights too, such as itinerant magicians, slackrope-walking toddlers and outlandishly decorated sacred bulls led around by their turbaned, *shennai*-blowing owners. The hawkers tend to wander home towards late afternoon, leaving the tourists and local fishermen casting lines into the surf to enjoy the sublime colours of the Goan sunset in relative peace.

50.715807, -1.876457
**BOURNEMOUTH,
UK**

At the height of summer, England's seaside resorts can be an assault on the senses, with the piercing screech of gulls, the ubiquitous aroma of takeaway fish and chips, and rows of saucy postcards and lobster-red flesh at every turn. And no self-respecting English seaside town is complete without its sticks of rock, donkey rides and, most importantly, a pier overloaded with gaudy amusements. Despite its unshakably genteel, old-fashioned image, Bournemouth is no exception to the rule, and with its pier overlooking one ot southern England's most pristine beaches, it's as good a place as any to pull up a deckchair, roll up your trousers and soak up the spectacle.

50.715807, -1.876457
ORTAKÖY, ISTANBUL,
TURKEY

You could be forgiven for thinking that swimming, tea-drinking and fishing are the Turkish national pastimes; along the shores of the Bosphorus, plenty of hours are unashamedly devoted to the enjoyment of each. Behind Ortaköy's eighteenth-century Büyük Mecidiye Mosque, Zuma, an outpost of London's finest Japanese restaurant, competes for custom with a slew of traditional waterfront cafés. Istanbul trendies trawl the nearby boutiques, while rowdy kids beat the heat with a splash around in the Bosphorus. Atatürk, modern Turkey's founding father, used to dive here too, but strong currents and waters teeming with jellyfish mean that taking the plunge is pretty much for experienced locals only.

29.227206, -81.006453
DAYTONA BEACH, FLORIDA, USA

For decades, Daytona Beach was invaded by half a million college kids going through the Spring Break ritual of underage drinking and libido liberation. In the mid-90s, the town ended its love affair with the nation's students and tried to cultivate a more refined image – an attempt that has been only partially successful, since nowadays it seems to cater mainly to bikers and race-car fanatics, and its rows of airbrushed t-shirt shops, amusement arcades, and wall-to-wall motels give it a decidedly seedy air. Without a doubt, the best thing about Daytona Beach is the beach itself: a seemingly limitless affair – 150m wide at low tide and fading dreamily into the heat haze. Most activity centres on the pier, where you can take the Sky Ride, a run-down cable car that ferries you slowly from one end of the pier to the other over the heads of patient anglers, or the Sky Coaster, a 100kph amusement ride to make your hair curl.

17.951019, -77.842893

**PELICAN BAR,
JAMAICA**

Jamaica's south coast offers varied pleasures, from gentle beach action at the terminally easy-going Treasure Beach to boat safaris in search of crocodiles and manatees on the Black River. Just east of here is the secluded fishing village of Parottee, where thanks to initiatives by hotels and enterprising locals, visitors are slowly arriving to explore nearby swamplands, go birdwatching, bask on golden-sand beaches and take boat tours to Pelican Bar – a ramshackle bird's-nest of a bar built on stilts in the middle of the sea. There are few more tranquil places to sample one of the island's award-winning rums or an ice-cold Red Stripe beer as you gaze out at a flaming Caribbean sunset.

37.799663, -112.409638
SAN FRANCISCO,
USA

San Francisco is most definitely not a place that welcomes large chains. Indeed, when Starbucks tried to oust a neighbourhood coffee shop a few years ago by buying the building and upping its rent, locals staged protests successful enough to scare the Seattle-based mega-roaster away and preserve the ramshackle café. The best selection of mom-and-pop cafés is to be found in the Mission and the Castro – both neighbourhoods where you'll be happy to linger over a latte – while North Beach still holds a clutch of traditional Italian cafés that serve delicious, spine-straightening espresso.

18.954685, 72.811530
**MUMBAI,
INDIA**

Chowpatty Beach is a Mumbai institution, which really comes to life at night and on Saturdays. People don't come here to swim – the sea is foul – but to wander, sit on the sand, have a massage, get their ears cleaned and gaze across the bay while the kids ride a pony or a rusty Ferris wheel. At one end of the beach, a row of *bhel puri* stalls hawk Mumbai's favourite sunset snack: crisp puffed rice with tamarind sauce, wrapped in a flat, fried *puri*.

46.992885, 21.981390
**BĂILE FELIX,
ROMANIA**

Romania boasts one third of all Europe's mineral springs, and around 160 spa resorts (*băile*) dot the country. But spa devotees shouldn't expect the usual five-star trappings: you're more likely to be slathered in foul-smelling mud than perfumed unguents, and there are no herbal tisanes to draw out those toxins either – treatments usually involve drinking the spa waters, which come in an amazing variety, from alkaline to iron-bearing, chlorinated to carbogaseous. You can't zone out while soaking in the hot springs either – you're encouraged to take healthy lungfuls of the pungent, sulphurous fumes as you bathe. Each spa has its own area of specialization; the waters of Băile Felix are believed to help with locomotive and rheumatic ailments, with treatments including healing mud baths, either in sapropelic fossil gunge or the local peat bog. Even if you decide to forego these treats, the thermal pool, set in parkland and surrounded by mock-rustic buildings, is a pleasant place for a dip: it's ted by the warm and slightly radioactive River Peţea, in which the thermal lotus thrives, otherwise found only in the Nile Delta.

36.685779, -6.137875

**JEREZ,
SPAIN**

The people of Jerez play a waiting game. They gather for idle chat in palm-laced plazas. They toy with tapas. They wait for June, when the workers head out into the sea of vineyards surrounding their whitewashed town to plant rows of young vines in the chalky soil, an absorbent loam that's perfect for producing the fine dry sherry the area is famous for. They seek shelter from the sun in the corner of forgotten squares. They take evening strolls through the old town. They wait for September, and the harvesting of the grapes, when the workers return with sackloads of juicy bunches to bless, press and then ferment in stainless steel vats until the end of November. They sit under bushes of floppy bougainvillea that grow plump and then fade. They watch the shadows lengthen. They wait for the sherry to age in oak barrels, dripping – a little at a time – from one barrel down to the next until, after at least three years, the first batch, the light, dry fino, is ready.

20.201892, -87.432793
**EL PARAÍSO BEACH CLUB,
TULUM, MEXICO**

Fronting a stretch of powdery, ochre-coloured sand, Tulum beach is one of the most inviting spots along the entire Riviera Maya. The El Paraíso resort, a few hundred metres from Tulum's archeological ruins, is as heavenly as its name promises, surrounded by a collection of palm trees and *porteros*, ready to pamper footsore sightseers descending from the ruins towering above. It can be tempting just to park yourself on a sun lounger and soak up your surroundings, but there are plenty of other ways to while away the hours here, not least dipping a toe in the uncannily warm waters – at 24°C in August and September, it can feel like kicking around in a warm bathtub. At the end of a long day's lounging, collapse on the club's enormous trampoline, just as the sun is setting and the doors opening for happy hour.

11.556589, 104.918082

**PHNOM PENH,
CAMBODIA**

Cyclo drivers are among the poorest of the working poor in Phnom Penh, drawn to the capital from all over Cambodia, looking for a way to earn extra riel between rice harvests. Many live on the street, kipping in their rented pedicabs at night, throwing a mosquito net over the awning, and snatching the occasional shady snooze in the midday heat. Others sleep in dorms at so-called cyclo houses. The city also has a dedicated welfare centre for cyclo drivers, the Cyclo Centre, which provides basic healthcare and support services. Phnom Penh's cyclo business is in decline as motorbike taxis and three-wheeled tuk-tuks steal away time-pressed passengers. But cyclos are still the handiest and most economical way to carry a big load back from market. And for visitors, they're the obvious, carbon-neutral answer to navigating the disorientating alleys of Cambodia's chaotic capital.

13.855789, -61.057913
**SOUFRIERE,
ST LUCIA**

All over the Caribbean, in wooden sheds with fresh breezes blowing through, in village rum shops or town squares, locals practise the time-honoured form of killing time, Caribbean-style: a game of dominoes. This is not child's play but a serious game for adults, played for money and pride, and with a concentration and energy quite remarkable for a game of such simplicity. Dominoes is especially popular with people who would otherwise spend a lot of time twiddling their thumbs: fishermen waiting to "pull in the seine" when their nets are full, or taxi drivers looking for something to do during the languid afternoon hours. You can usually tell when a game is in progress: you'll hear shouting and the clacking of tiles or "bones" being slapped down on the table as players try to intimidate opponents, or in exuberant celebration. St Lucia, Jamaica, Barbados, The Bahamas and Cuba are among the islands that embrace this domino culture, though emigration has exported it to Miami and further afield. The game that keeps the drowsy island afternoon awake is also played competitively, and the Caribbean is always well represented in world domino championships.

Tourist trail

I had started the morning in Oscar Wilde's bedroom, lying on the bed, trying to find an angle to shoot the gorgeous peacock wallpaper without too much reflection. Next, I popped by to see *Mona Lisa*. Tired of the endless tourists, she barely smiled. My brief was to turn the camera on the snappers! There were some puzzled expressions and a few huffs and puffs, but I stood my ground in a prime position up against the rope until I got my shot. An hour later, I was stalking a fur-coated lady walking a tiny dog in St-Germaine. A bizarre day's work? No, just your average day as a Rough Guides photographer, ticking off items on the all-important picture list.

Lydia Evans, *Photographer for The Rough Guide to Paris*

48.860833, 2.336740
**PARIS,
FRANCE**

The Musée du Louvre is crammed with masterpieces, but few visitors are able to resist the allure of the *Mona Lisa*, if only to see what all the fuss is about. Leonardo's most famous painting now receives some six million visitors a year, but this small, dark sixteenth-century portrait remained neglected for years, only really hitting the big time when she was stolen by a security guard in August 1911. By the time she was recovered, in December 1913, the *Mona Lisa*'s face had graced the pages of endless books and newspapers. Since then, celebrity has fed on itself, and she now faces more flashguns every day than a well-dressed starlet on Oscar night. The *Mona Lisa*'s fame has swelled yet further as a result of her bit-part appearance in Dan Brown's *The Da Vinci Code*, though visitors are sometimes as unimpressed as Brown's heroine Sophie Neveu, who finds the painting "too little" and "foggy". Basically, it's filthy – no art restorer has yet dared to work on the picture – but if you can struggle past the crowds, the dirt of centuries and your own familiarity with the image, you might just discover a strange and beautiful painting.

25.795410, -80.127513
MIAMI,
USA

For a place built on holidays and hype, Miami lives up to, and revels in, the clichés: the people on the beach are indeed as tanned and toned as they are on TV; the weather seldom dips below balmy; the cafés are full of aspiring models; and the nightlife is pumping and hedonistic. A gorgeous, gaudy place, the city abounds with lazy palm trees, and its wide, golden beaches are spacious enough to seem empty even on a sweltering Sunday in high season. The Setai Hotel on Collins Avenue, known for its celebrity-heavy clientele as much as for its high-priced, vaguely Asian-themed rooms, is a suitably chichi place for a spot of poolside lounging, Miami-style.

26.987779, 75.854448
AMBER FORT, RAJASTHAN, INDIA

Just south of Jaipur, in the state of Rajasthan, lies the magnificent Amber Fort, an imposing line of royal palaces, temples and fortresses which straggle along the summit of a spectacularly craggy and inaccessible hilltop – one of the region's most dramatic citadels. Most modern visitors opt to walk up the steep road to the fort, though those wishing to make the ascent in the manner of a true maharaja can hire their own elephant for the leisurely climb up to the palace gates, sitting atop a colourful howdah on the back of one of these mighty beasts, while a turbaned mahout goads and encourages his charge up the challenging ascent. For a taste of traditional India the ride has few peers, offering wonderful elephant-back views over the surrounding countryside, as well as a certain sense of regal power, as your majestic mount climbs sedately upwards, sending pedestrians fleeing for cover, and depositing large mounds of elephant dung en route.

35.714701, 139.796761

SENSO-JI TEMPLE, ASAKUSA, TOKYO, JAPAN

For centuries now, the approach to Tokyo's oldest temple has been lined with colourful shops. In the beginning they served religious men, weary from months on the road, but now they cater for pilgrims of a very different kind. Every day, thousands of tourists clamber up from the subway and out onto the streets of ancient Asakusa, dodging geishas, smog and rickshaws, before swarming around the vast paper lantern that swings from Thunder Gate. This is the entrance to Senso-ji temple – one of the city's most important Buddhist monuments – and the first port of call for snap-happy visitors. From here they enter the Nakamise-dori, a 200-metre-long shopping street that sparkles with polythene-wrapped gifts. There are manga t-shirts and bright red lollipops laid out alongside the latest mobile phone trinkets. Bags of freshly cooked rice crackers are snapped up by Japanese day-trippers, and foreign tourists queue for the traditional *omikuji* scrolls that are said to predict fortunes. At the far end of the thoroughfare an enormous black cauldron chugs incense into the sky, drawing new worshippers to the temple and bestowing health on those already there. In the haze of it all, capitalism and religion become one.

27.745246, -15.576492

MASPALOMAS, GRAN CANARIA

At Gran Canaria's southern tip, vast drifts of pristine golden sand pile up to form the shimmering dunes of Maspalomas, the centrepiece of the resort complex known as the Costa Canaria. Half a century ago, this was a lonely stretch of coast backed by semi-arid farmland, neglected for most of its history and once the haunt of European and North African pirates. But in 1961 Count Alejandro del Castillo, the enterprising local landowner, organized a competition to create a new resort, sparking a tourist gold rush. Hotels and apartment blocks, leafy bungalow complexes and stark concrete shopping centres soon engulfed the sleepy village of Maspalomas (whose name means simply "more pigeons"), and sun, sea, sand and pulsating nightlife have been provided with ruthless efficiency ever since.

38.889262, -77.050102
**WASHINGTON DC,
USA**

One of the USA's most recognizable symbols, the Lincoln Memorial is regularly appropriated – in oratory and backdrop – by politicians of all stripes to advance policies that may or may not have anything to do with the legacy of the 16th president. It's perhaps most famous as the backdrop to Dr Martin Luther King Jr's "I Have a Dream" speech on August 28, 1963, delivered to 200,000 people. Almost half a century later, on January 20, 2009 – the day after Martin Luther King Day and some 200 years after Lincoln's birth – it hosted Barack Obama's inauguration. The president-elect, who arrived on these steps following a train ride that traced Lincoln's own inaugural path from Philadelphia to Washington, was greeted by a jubilant crowd of some two million supporters. Even when there's no president to gawp at, the memorial provides a stirring backdrop for photographs, and climbing the steps to meet the seated Lincoln's steely gaze is one of DC's most profound experiences.

36.617999, -121.901566

**CALIFORNIA,
USA**

During World War II, Monterey was the sardine capital of the western world, catching and canning some 200,000 tonnes of the fish each year. However, overfishing meant that by 1945 business had more or less dried up, and the canneries were abandoned, falling into disrepair until the 1970s, when they were converted into shopping malls and flashy restaurants. The area received a further boost with the opening of the magnificent Monterey Bay Aquarium in 1984 – one of the largest, most stunning displays of underwater life in the world. Some 1.8 million visitors a year press their noses against the vast windows of the aquarium's tank to gaze at the species that populate the deep waters just beyond the bay. Lazy hammerhead sharks glide amongst foul-tempered tuna, while barracuda dart past and massive sunfish weighing up to a ton make their stately circuit of the tank perimeter.

29.555465, 35.443182
**WADI RUM,
JORDAN**

The compact Hashemite kingdom of Jordan is one of the best places to go trekking in the Middle East. In the north, you can wander through thickets of pistachio and olive trees, and meadows carpeted with spring flowers. Just off the central Kings Highway, trails follow the course of the craggy Wadi Mujib gorge as it scythes through scorched earth and down towards the Dead Sea. But it's amongst the scattered monoliths of Wadi Rum, in the far south, that the stark beauty of the country really soaks into your soul. And getting out into the desert has never been so easy: from Rum's Visitor Centre, a network of routes crisscrosses the desert floor and runs up, over or around eroded plateaus and rust-red cliffs. A bevy of local guides can lead you on foot to the towering hulk of Jebel Rum, and Ain Shalaaleh, a lush, shady spring known to Lawrence of Arabia; or out through the canyons of Jebel Umm Ashreen to scale the wind-sculpted dunes of Wadi Umm Ashreen. Or you could always head off into the desert yourself: a few minutes' walk from the centre in any direction and it'll be just you and the vast, echoing landscape.

19.665287, -90.419304

**HACIENDA UAYAMON,
YUCATÁN, MEXICO**

Deep in Mexico's southeast, flanked to the east by the
clear blue waters of the Caribbean and the Gulf of Mexico,
lies the sublime Yucatán peninsula. The ancient seat of
the Mayan civilizations is now better known to many for
the all-inclusive resorts and clutch of stupendous bikini-
and-Bermuda beaches of Cancún, at the peninsula's
northernmost tip. You could walk these satiny sands for
weeks and still not reach the end – the Yucatán is blessed
with hundreds of kilometres of beach – but if you're looking
for peace and quiet, steer clear of Cancún's spring-breakers
and head for the colonial town of Campeche instead. On
the Gulf coast of the peninsula, this pastel-painted haven is
surrounded by ancient sites, and makes an appealing place
to hole up for a few days, whether in a simple guesthouse
or a five-star hacienda such as the Uayamon: the perfect
antidote to Cancún's high-rises.

27.790320, -15.724000
**PLAYA DE AMADORES,
GRAN CANARIA, SPAIN**

Birds of a feather flock together on the sandy beach of
Playa de Amadores, in the southwest of the Canary Island of
Gran Canaria, where each winter thousands of sun-starved
northern Europeans mimic the continent's bird population
and fly south to avoid the worst of the northern winter.
They find the escape they crave in the Canaries' spring-like
temperatures and almost guaranteed sunshine. The purpose-
built resort and artificial beach of Amadores, crammed with
sun-baked bodies, may lack authentic Canarian charm, but
the dazzling white apartments that climb its hillsides and
the hypnotic effect of the endless rows of beach umbrellas
nevertheless create their own visual drama. Mass tourism
brought prosperity to the island in the 1960s and 1970s, but
as competition from more fashionable destinations increases
the island has upped its game, investing in luxurious new
hotels and vaunting the charms of its unspoilt mountainous
interior, hoping to attract a different breed of holidaymaker,
for whom the serried ranks of Amadores' beach umbrellas
would be holiday hell.

37.728341, -119.573286
**GLACIER POINT,
YOSEMITE, USA**

Right from the early days of tourism in Yosemite, Glacier Point's combination of boulders, pines and granite-formed viewpoints held an irresistible allure, but from the early twentieth century to the late 1960s, the area's biggest draw was the spectacular Firefall. Every summer evening at the end of Camp Curry's evening entertainment programme, guests gazed up at Glacier Point, 975m above, where a fire made from ten barrow-loads of red fir bark could be seen lighting up the night sky. As the show drew to a close, the stentorian voice of camp owner David Curry would boom out "Hello Glacier! Is the fire ready?" The faint reply of "The fire is ready!" would waft back down, and at Curry's instruction "Let the Fire Fall!" the smouldering embers would be raked over the cliff to create a 300-metre fiery cascade that seemed to fall almost directly on the guests. The event was so popular that spectacle-seekers crossed counties, clogged Valley roads and trampled meadows to stake out the best vantage points. Though the cinders never caused a serious fire, the Firefall was eventually deemed inappropriate for a national park. The last one took place on Jan 25, 1968, but park rangers still delight in telling the tale.

43.769591, 11.255600

**FLORENCE,
ITALY**

No country in Europe is more photogenic than Italy. From the jagged peaks of the Dolomites in the north, through the ancient hill-towns of Tuscany to the lava wilderness of Sicily's Mount Etna, its richness and variety hold endless appeal for visitors. Then there's the art; throw a dart at a map of Italy and you can hardly fail to hit a spot that's close to a masterpiece or two. In Florence, there's almost too much to see; the city has been synonymous with art-overload every since Stendhal reeled around its streets, dazed by the likes of Giotto, Botticelli, Donatello, Michelangelo, Leonardo da Vinci and Raphael. Michelangelo's *David* has become the most-photographed statue in the world – though the version in this picture is a copy. The original, housed in the Accademia gallery, ensures a lengthy queue at the entrance every morning – but you can expect an even longer line outside the Uffizi, Italy's finest collection of Renaissance art. The gallery attracts 1.5 million visitors per year – that's almost four times the population of Florence.

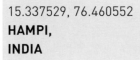
15.337529, 76.460552

**HAMPI,
INDIA**

The Indian tradition of pilgrimage dates back for millennia, and remains a popular occupation today among all sections of Indian society, from wandering Hindu *saddhus* and Jain monks who spend their lives walking barefoot across the country from shrine to shrine, begging for sustenance en route, to the more modern pilgrims, who tear between temples in specially chartered video buses, combining the high-speed accrual of religious merit with sightseeing and shopping. Among a surreal landscape of golden-brown boulders and leafy banana fields, the ruined "City of Victory," Vijayanagar, better known as Hampi, spills from the south bank of the River Tungabhadra, a location long considered sacred by Hindus. The serene river setting and air of magic that lingers over the site, sacred for centuries before a city was founded here, make it one of India's most extraordinary locations, drawing a steady flow of pilgrims from all over southern India.

36.168239, -115.138484
**LAS VEGAS,
USA**

Las Vegas has always had a ruthless streak. Ever since mobster Bugsy Siegel was gunned down by his erstwhile partners in 1947 – his newly opened Flamingo was making money, it just wasn't making it fast enough – the city has been desperately chasing the next buck, happy to discard its past without a backward glance. The rough-and-ready frontier town squeezed itself into a tux when Frank Sinatra and his Rat Pack ruled the roost, slipped into a toga when the 1960s turned decadent, and even slapped on the greasepaint during its brief bid to re-invent itself as a great place to bring the kids. These days, a handful of giant corporations own every casino in town. Everything is bigger and shinier than ever, and the new watchwords seem to be sophistication, elegance and opulence. What little old-style neon still survives lies well away from the Strip, appealing now largely to nostalgics who feel the modern city has strayed too far from the no-nonsense populism of its early years. There's even a "Neon Boneyard", where you can pay your respects to long-abandoned neon masterpieces – assuming you can tear yourself away from the gaming tables.

28.398486, 83.688354
**THE HIMALAYA,
NEPAL**

The dramatic Annapurna region, north of the tourist hub of Pokhara, has long been one of Nepal's most popular trekking destinations. Covering a 40km stretch of the Himalaya, the mighty Annapurna Himal harbours nine jutting peaks over 7000m, and is crisscrossed with challenging treks. Early in the morning at Annapurna Base Camp (a mere 4130m up), as the sun inches over the black ridge above, bleary-eyed trekkers get their cameras out to capture the gradual illumination of Annapurna I – at 8091m, a legend among climbers in that it was the first eight-thousand-metre peak to be conquered. In recent years, however, the construction of new roads has had a significant impact on some of the trekking routes, with the classic three-week Annapurna Circuit now effectively rendered obsolete. Guides have been forced to stake out different routes and explore new areas, such as Dolpo, home to the elusive snow leopard and a magical, isolated place – at least for now.

40.751317, 14.487013

**POMPEII,
ITALY**

Some two thousand citizens perished in the AD 79 eruption of Vesuvius, asphyxiated by toxic fumes, their homes buried beneath volcanic ash and pumice. Pompeii is a remarkable record of a town stopped in its tracks, and a visit here will give you more of a sense of the lives of ordinary ancient Romans than any history book could. Coachloads of sightseers pound Pompeii's ancient cobblestones every day, photographing its chipped mosaics and fading frescoes, trooping around the remains of its elegant villas and sniggering at the erotic art in its ancient brothel. But Pompeii is now at risk of eradication for a second time: centuries of foot traffic and the ravages of the elements are taking their toll, and mismanagement and lack of investment have left priceless relics uncared-for. Buildings and artefacts that were preserved by Vesuvius' volcanic ash are now in disrepair, with at least 150 square metres of fresco and plasterwork lost each year. Such is the danger that in 2008 the Italian government declared a state of emergency in a bid to preserve what's left.

Ever since its days as a Dutch trading post in the early seventeenth century, countless people have tried their luck in New York's Financial District on Manhattan's southern tip. Fortunes have been won and blown on Wall Street, which, following the creation of the New York Stock Exchange in 1817, evolved into the centre of American and international business. While the manic activity on the Exchange floor is no longer open to the public for security reasons, following the attacks on the nearby World Trade Center in 2001, you can partake of the traders' good luck ritual involving the Wall Street Bull. A three-and-half-tonne bronze sculpture symbolizing the bull (or rising) market, this colossal statue was hauled by truck into the city by guerilla artist Arturo di Modica in 1989 and left without permission outside the Exchange. It was subsequently moved to its current location around the corner on Bowling Green, where the bull's enormous balls are rubbed by luck-seeking visitors and traders alike, as their impressive burnish attests.

51.5111, -0.123913
COVENT GARDEN, LONDON, UK

It is a city of grand monuments and vigorous culture, but London is also a city of tat. Bad taste abounds: dubious national symbols are printed on gaudy cards, free newspapers crammed with celebrity nothings litter the streets and tourists browse stands of t-shirts covered in jokes so bad they wouldn't make it into a Christmas cracker. It is tempting to say that all this is new, a symptom of a declining power with decaying tastes, but that would ignore a long and proud tradition of cheesy cheer, from the music hall and Punch and Judy through Penny Dreadfuls and Benny Hill. The tacky shops and heaving pavements of London's West End are as much a part of the city as the airy Tate Modern or leafy Regent's Park, and the clichéd images on postcards, to be slipped in those iconic red postboxes, propped up on mantelpieces or lost in a mess of socks at the back of a suitcase, are bullet points in Britain's identity. They might not show us as we'd like to be, but in their vulgarity, their irony and their fascination with history, place and class, they give a surprisingly good sense of who we are.

37.419084, 127.456384
KOREAN FOLK VILLAGE, KOREA

The Korean Folk Village, an hour from Seoul, has become one of the most popular tourist draws in the area, its thatch-roofed houses and dirt paths evoking the sights, sounds and some of the more pleasant smells of a bygone time, when farming was the mainstay of the country. Here, the emphasis is squarely on performance – shows of seesaw-jumping (a traditional village game that remains popular in modern-day Korea), tightrope-walking and horseriding take place regularly throughout the day. A re-creation of a traditional wedding ceremony provides a glimpse into Confucian society, with painstaking attention to detail including gifts of live chickens wrapped up in cloth like Egyptian mummies. And don't miss the farmers' dance, in which costumed performers prance around in highly distinctive ribbon-topped hats amid a cacophony of drums and crashes – quintessential Korea.

40.748696, -73.985742
**NEW YORK CITY,
USA**

Easily the most potent and evocative symbol of New York, the building that King Kong clung to while grabbing at passing aircraft is still the most original and elegant skyscraper of them all. From toe to TV mast, the Empire State Building is 102 storeys and 443m tall, but its height is deceptive, rising in stately tiers with steady panache. In a city filled with world-class attractions, the Empire State Building is still top of most people's list; every day, hordes of tourists take the lift to the 86th-floor outdoor walkways, to gaze at the legendary views for themselves.

20.508872, -87.719479
**NOHOCH MUL,
YUCATÁN, MEXICO**

If you'd climbed the looming Nohoch Mul twenty years ago, chances are you'd have had only monkeys and birds for company. Today, thanks to the explosive growth of Cancún and the Riviera Maya, coach tours flood the site of Cobá from the early morning and there's almost always a crowd enjoying the shade at the foot of the pyramid, recovering from the climb or psyching themselves up for the attempt. Perhaps because it is surrounded by lofty forest trees, the pyramid doesn't immediately look that impressive, but once you start to climb the narrow, precipitous and mercilessly shadeless stairway you quickly appreciate just how big it is. Once at the temple at the top, though, you're amply rewarded: taking in nearby lakes as well as jungle stretching uninterrupted to the horizon, the views from up here are nothing short of awe-inspiring.

20.355542, 100.080777
**SOP RUAK,
THAILAND**

This gleaming, golden Buddha, perched atop a modern temple in the village of Sop Ruak, northern Thailand, seems to rise serenely above the gaudy commercialism of the notorious Golden Triangle below. Coined to denote a huge opium-producing area spreading across Burma, Laos and Thailand, the Golden Triangle has, for the benefit of tourists, been artificially concentrated into the precise spot where the borders meet, at the confluence of the Ruak and Mekong rivers, 70km northeast of Chiang Rai. Don't come to Sop Ruak expecting to run into sinister drug-runners, or even poppy fields – instead you'll find souvenir stalls, two opium museums and countless "Golden Triangle" signs, which pop up in a million photo albums around the world.

41.906553, 12.454022
**ROME,
ITALY**

The Vatican Museums amount to the largest, richest, most compelling and perhaps most exhausting collection of art in the world: a set of museums so stuffed with antiquities as to put most other European collections to shame. The queues that snake around the Vatican walls are almost legendary – wilting under a relentless Roman sun for hours on end before stepping into the museums' hallowed coolness is all part of the experience. Once inside, you have a choice of routes, so decide how long you want to spend here, and what you want to see, before you start. One-way routes allow for anything from a day-long trek round the seven kilometres of galleries to a flying visit to the Sistine Chapel – reducing the risk of museum fatigue.

43.080220, -79.075835

**NIAGARA FALLS,
USA**

Every second, almost three-quarters of a million gallons of water explode over the knife-edge Niagara Falls – an awesome spectacle that's made even more impressive by the variety of methods laid on to help you get closer to it: boats, walkways, observation towers and helicopters all push as near to the curtains of gushing water as they dare. At night, the falls are lit up, and the coloured waters tumble dramatically into blackness, while in winter the whole scene changes as the falls freeze to form gigantic razor-tipped icicles. The nineteenth-century tightrope-walker Blondin crossed the Niagara repeatedly, and even carried passengers across on his back, while others over the years have taken the plunge in barrels; remarkably, ten of the fifteen survived the fall. The reason such craziness has long been banned becomes self-evident when you approach the towering cascade on the *Maid of the Mist*, which has been ferrying passengers through Niagara's dense mist of spray since 1846.

-2.108899, 34.843140
THE SERENGETI, TANZANIA

Once a year, some 2.5 million wildebeest, zebra and other animals move north from the Serengeti plains into Kenya's Maasai Mara Game Reserve, following the life-giving rains – with hungry lions and hyenas never far behind. One of nature's most awe-inspiring displays, the migration has long been a source of fascination for visitors, but these days, tourists accustomed to the sweeping aerial shots of glossy wildlife documentaries want to take in the spectacle from all angles. From inflation and lift-off at dawn to the (often bumpy) landing, a hot-air balloon provides the perfect roost from which to view the migration, reducing the galloping mass below to something resembling a teeming ant's nest.

Tradition

After a few days of shooting the Rough Guide to Orlando, all the huge, over-crowded theme parks had started to blend together, and I was glad to head out to the small town of Mount Dora with my camera. The owner of the Windsor Rose tearoom suggested I speak to the two elderly ladies who were sitting at the window table. I went over, apologized for interrupting their tea and asked if I might take a few snaps of their table. They were thrilled, and were happy to chat while I snapped away. Once I had the image I needed, I thanked them, declined their gracious offer to join them for tea and headed back to the city for shots of roller coasters and thumping nightclubs.

Dan Bannister, *Photographer for The Rough Guide to Orlando*

28.799467, -81.64537
MOUNT DORA, FLORIDA, USA

The quaint old houses and antiques shops might bring to mind an English village, but in spite of its location, in theme-park-heavy Florida, Mount Dora is as authentic as they come. This Victorian-era village on a pristine lake, nestled amongst the gentle hills and orange groves of central Florida, has its fair share of English-style traditions – it would be sacrilegious to come here and not partake of tea and scones at one of the many tearooms dotted around town. The genteel Windsor Rose Tea Room serves these and other favourites from across the pond – from cucumber sandwiches and Victoria sponge cake to Cornish pasties and Scotch eggs – on nostalgically doily-draped tables.

15.409124, -91.147428
**NEBAJ,
GUATEMALA**

Textile weaving is arguably the great craft tradition in the Maya highlands of Guatemala. Nebaj, set in a vast bowl-shaped valley, is one of the three towns of Ixil, a deeply traditional area of around 120,000 people where Spanish is very much a second language. Here the backstrap loom (used by the ancient Maya) is still king, and virtually every woman will put aside an hour or two a day to thread together a *huipil* (blouse) or one of the spectacular turbanesque headdresses that define the town's costume and Maya identity. For fiestas and special events the streets are a blaze of colour as astonishingly intricate *huipils* and ceremonial costumes are showcased. The relaxed nature of the people and colour of the scene disguises a deeply troubled past, for Ixil was one of the areas worst affected by Guatemala's 36-year civil war that claimed 200,000 (mainly Maya) lives.

17.994868, -66.621265
PONCE,
PUERTO RICO

Ponce holds Puerto Rico's oldest and most dazzling Carnaval, opening with a procession led by King Momo (the traditional "King of Carnivals") and figures known as *vejigantes*, mostly local boys whose ornate masks are embellished with outlandish colours and devilish horns. The original purpose of the *vejigante* was to scare people – they traditionally represented Moorish warriors – and these days you'll see them merrily thwacking kids that line the streets with a *vejiga*, a dried cow's bladder blown up like a balloon. The merrymaking ends on Shrove Tuesday with the bizarre Entierro de la Sardina (Burial of the Sardine), a mock funeral procession attended by hyperbolic cries and wails from everyone in sight. A fish is symbolically burnt at the climax, signifying the purging of sins before the beginning of Lent.

35.696934, 139.793488

**NATIONAL SUMO STADIUM,
RYÐGOKU, JAPAN**

There's something fascinating about sumo, Japan's national sport. The age-old pomp and ceremony that surrounds the titanic clashes between enormous, near-naked wrestlers – from the design of the *dohy* (the ring in which bouts take place) to the wrestler's slicked-back topknot – give the sport a gravitas completely absent from Western wrestling. Accounts of sumo bouts date back around 2000 years when it was a Shinto rite connected with praying for a good harvest. Later, sumo developed into a spectator sport, but the old religious trappings remain: the *gyoji* (referee) wears robes similar to those of a Shinto priest, and above the *dohy* hangs a thatched roof like those found at shrines. At the start of a bout the two *rikishi* (wrestlers) wade into the ring, wearing only *mawashi* aprons, which are essentially giant jock-straps. Salt is tossed to purify the ring, and then the *rikishi* hunker down and indulge in the time-honoured ritual of psyching each other out with menacing stares. When ready, each *rikishi* attempts to throw his opponent to the ground or out of the ring using one or more of 82 legitimate techniques. The first to touch the ground with any part of his body other than his feet, or to step out of the *dohy*, loses.

15.257098, 73.918655
**BENAULIM,
GOA**

According to Hindu mythology, Goa was created when the sage Shri Parasurama, Vishnu's sixth incarnation, fired an arrow into the sea from the top of the Western Ghats and ordered the waters to recede. The spot where the shaft fell to earth, known in Sanskrit as Banali ("place where the arrow landed") and later corrupted by the Portuguese to Benaulim, lies in the dead centre of Colva beach, surrounded by coconut groves and paddy fields, and is hard to beat as a place to unwind. The beach is breathtaking, particularly around sunset, when its brilliant white sand and churning surf reflect the changing colours to magical effect. It's also lined with Goa's largest and most colourfully decorated fleet of wooden outriggers, which provide welcome shade during the heat of the day.

51.516594, -0.209481

**LONDON,
UK**

Once a year in August, Notting Hill's peaceful old streets are transformed into a wash of colour, sound, movement and the pure, unadulterated joy that makes Carnival the festival highlight of London's party calendar. On Sunday morning, sound-system guys, still bleary-eyed from the excesses of last night's warm-up parties, wire up their towering stacks of speakers, while fragrant smoke wafts from the stalls of early-bird jerk chicken chefs. And then a bass line trembles through the morning air, and the trains begin to disgorge crowds of revellers, dressed to impress and brandishing their whistles and horns. Some head straight for the sound systems, spending the day moving from one to the other and stopping wherever the music takes them. But the backbone of Carnival is mas, the parade of costumed bands that threads its way through the centre of the event. Crowds line up along the route and the whole area becomes a seething throng of floats and flags, sequins and feathers, as the mas bands cruise along, their revellers dancing up a storm to the tunes bouncing from the music trucks. And for the next two days, the only thing that matters is the delicious, anarchic freedom of dancing on the streets of London.

-34.620454, -58.371783
**BUENOS AIRES,
ARGENTINA**

In Buenos Aires, tango is a world unto itself (*el mundo tanguero*). Most visitors tend to associate tango with dance – partly thanks to the Hollywood image of Rudolph Valentino tossing his partner around, a rose in his teeth. Yet tango is a complete art form: part seduction, part performance, it's a combination of music, poetry and scintillating footwork – sometimes brash, occasionally vulgar, but often elegant and always mesmerizing. The accompanying music gets its distinctive sound – the bloodcurdling tone of longing – from the *bandoneón*, a German cousin of the accordion and the concertina; the melancholy groan, acidic timbre and sliding rhythm are a perfect match for tango.

**KERALA,
INDIA**

Experiencing Keralan ritual theatre in its authentic context – against a backdrop of flickering coconut-oil lamps in a temple courtyard, with the ancient rhythms of Vedic chants and *chenda* drums filling the night air – is about the closest you can come to time travel. The adventures of god-heroes and their demonic adversaries are the most common subjects of *kathakali* story-plays, Kerala's most popular and best-known ritual art form, which have been enacted in the same way for thousands of years. Whether goodies, baddies, superheroes with special powers or female consorts, each of the four main character types wears instantly recognizable, and equally outlandish, costumes. Ridged masks of rice paper, decorative headgear set with red and green stones and voluminous skirts and jewellery adorn the "green" (*pacha*) heroes. Audiences, however, tend to most enjoy the antics of the villainous, lustful, greedy and violent "knife" (*katti*) anti-heroes, with their fangs and red-and-black faces.

22.543454, 104.294930

BAC HA,
VIETNAM

Vietnam boasts the richest and most complex ethnic make-up in Southeast Asia. Some eleven million people belong to fifty-two minority groups, themselves comprising dozens of subgroups. Most live in Vietnam's marginal mountainous regions, where the poorer and more isolated tribes preserve their time-honoured ways of life, including a dazzling array of traditional costumes, particularly in the north. From an early age, girls learn how to weave and make fine brocades, gradually building up a collection of dresses and blankets to form part of their dowry; a girl's skill at weaving increases her chances of making a good match. Watching women from the Flower Hmong hill tribe rifle through stalls for the perfect accessory is well worth the ride up to the Sunday market in Bac Ha. These tribeswomen have an extraordinarily fancy taste in clothes, with a particular penchant for machine-embroidered brocades in eye-popping shades such as camellia pink and lime green.

18.467394, -66.117182
**SAN JUAN,
PUERTO RICO**

Puerto Rico is an island of immigrants, its dynamic criollo blend of African, European, Taíno and American traditions expressed through a seemingly endless list of festivals celebrated with passion by the whole community. Though many have Spanish roots, Puerto Rican fiestas have become deliciously localized, its lively street parties marked with an unmistakable Caribbean twist. The most festive period to be in San Juan is over the Christmas holidays, when you'll hear live music everywhere, especially performances of *aguinaldos*, a type of Christmas folk music unique to the island, but based on traditional Spanish carols. On January 6 crowds gather in Old San Juan for Three Kings Day, when the governor hands out presents to children, while at the San Sebastián Street Festival, held over three days at the end of January, the whole town gets together to see off the holiday season in true Puerto Rican style: with singing, dancing and a flamboyant procession through the streets.

39.906293, 116.397539
**BEIJING,
CHINA**

Making kites is an ancient Chinese art, but Beijing, Tianjin and Weifang are particularly prized for their designs. The first kite-maker is thought to have been a Chinese philosopher called Mo-tse in around 230 BC, who laboured over the design for his wooden eagle for three years before he could get it to fly. Though originally a pursuit that only the wealthy could afford to indulge in — the use of materials such as silk made kite-flying an expensive hobby — the invention of paper meant that ordinary people could join in too. Kites developed into complex 3D shapes, which were elaborately decorated and flown on ceremonial occasions to bring good luck. Today, kite-flying is seasonal, starting at the beginning of the Chinese New Year and ending around April when the winds blow yellow dust from the deserts to the north of Beijing.

-34.156989, -70.744636

CENTRAL VALLEY, CHILE

The birthplace and heartland of Chilean rodeo is the Central Valley – by far the best place to get up close to the incredible displays of horsemanship put on by the *huasos*. These Chilean cowboys cut a dashing figure with their bright, finely woven ponchos, broad-rimmed hats, carved wooden stirrups and shining silver spurs. In the main part of a rodeo, pairs of *huasos* drive a young cow around the edge of the arena and pin it up against a padded section of the wall. The teamwork between horses and riders is breathtaking, with one keeping as close to the rear of the cow as possible while the other gallops sideways, keeping his horse's chest close to the cow's front shoulders. When they reach the cushion, the object is to bring the cow to a sudden stop and hold it up against the wall until the judges have awarded points for style.

36.539059, 128.516704

HAHOE FOLK VILLAGE, KOREA

Despite its rapid economic growth, Korea's pastoral traditions are alive and well – nowhere more so than in the preserved folk villages dotted around the country. While some exist purely for show, others are functioning communities where life dawdles on at an intentionally slow pace, the residents surviving on a curious mix of home-grown vegetables, government subsidy and tourist-generated income. Hahoe Folk Village is one of the best and most popular in the country, a charming tangle of over a hundred countryside houses nestling in the gentle embrace of an idle river. This mix of mud walls and thatched roofs makes an evocative location for performances of Hahoe Pyolshingut Talnori, an age-old masked dance which has been designated Important Intangible Cultural Asset #69 by the government. The dance features nine different masked personalities – such as a monk, scholar, butcher and old woman – and uses humour and satire to ease tensions between the different social classes.

39.903317, 116.383023
**BEIJING,
CHINA**

Decked out in an elaborate costume and under a thick layer of make-up, Chinese opera performers use gesture, song, dance and martial arts in a highly stylized performance, whose every aspect is codified by convention and full of symbolism. Walking in a circle represents a long journey; to flick the sleeves means anger; upturned palms denotes embarrassment; and a character about to speak adjusts his headdress. The actor's aim is to instil beauty in every gesture, and, as in the forms of t'ai chi, to make smooth, sweeping, rounded movements and avoid the angular and abrupt. And all, of course, must be done in time to the din of percussive music.

39.469757, -0.376349

**VALENCIA,
SPAIN**

The people of Valencia celebrate their patron saint's day and the passing of winter with a fiery party of ferocious proportions: ground-shaking fire-cracker fights, rockets booming overhead, billowing clouds of sulphurous smoke, and colossal bonfires on street corners that could cook your eyeballs from twenty metres. The main feature of Valencia's famous festival is the *fallas* effigies themselves, which come in all shapes and sizes, the most spectacular of them being enormous affairs. Almost four hundred are erected around the city, and as many as four hundred more in the surrounding towns and districts. Combine all this with the Spanish love of sangria, bravado and all-hours partying, and you get one hell of an early spring line-up that draws two million people from all over the world.

-22.910958, -43.196762
RIO DE JANEIRO, BRAZIL

If you thought Rio's Carnival (Carnaval in Portuguese) was just a three-day affair, think again. In no other country is the unbridled pursuit of pleasure such a national obsession, and Carnaval's status as the most important celebration on the Brazilian calendar – easily outstripping Christmas and Easter – entails preparing more or less the whole year in advance. Rio's samba schools recruit supporters in their thousands to help create the impossibly glitzy costumes, while flamboyant dances are choreographed by the *carnavelesco*, the school's director. During Carnaval itself, the city shuts up shop and throws itself into the most dazzling spectacle you're ever likely to see. Some 50,000 people take part in the no-holds-barred, all-night *desfiles* (parades): a spectacular piece of street theatre unmatched anywhere else on earth. In a place riven by poverty, the festival represents a moment of freedom and release, when the aspirations of Rio's citizens can be expressed in music and song.

51.508334, -0.136404
LONDON, UK

It's the fittings – the dark wood, frosted windows and shining brass, the fruit machine tinkling with measured merriment, the hand pumps and the spirits standing to attention at the bar – that define the classic pub. But it's the customers who create the atmosphere. They crowd in their exuberant scores after work, full of gossip and grumbles and hellos and goodbyes, and mill contentedly at the weekend, eyeing up the football scores, the menu and each other. After all the hubbub, a visit at a quieter time – a Tuesday afternoon, or early on a Sunday – can feel like a vast sigh of relief. The bar staff are friendlier and the tables invitingly empty. Papers can be read and drinks – like Pride and ESB, two fine ales brewed in London – savoured. Many pubs have their origins as 1830s beer houses, their opening encouraged by a government keen to wean the working classes off gin, their bars set in the parlours of the ordinary houses of enterprising citizens. You might have a ball on those intoxicating, busy evenings, but visit in fallow times and you'll feel right at home.

38.118751, 13.370552
**PALERMO,
ITALY**

In Palermo, puppetry isn't just for kids – puppet theatre has been a traditional Sicilian entertainment for people of all ages since the fourteenth century. All Sicilians know the stories, which centre on the clash between Christianity and Islam, and performances are rowdy – usually tales of battles in shouted dialect – and often staged in backstreet puppet theatres which have been run by the same families for generations. As the strutting, stiff-legged knight is introduced – Orlando (Roland), more often than not – the puppeteer lists his exploits. There may be a love interest, and perhaps a jousting tournament to win the hand of Charlemagne's daughter, before the main business of staged battles between the Christians and the Saracen invaders begins.

37.369813, -6.000305

**SEVILLE,
SPAIN**

Held in Seville barely two weeks after the Easter festivities, the Feria de Abril is the country's largest fair – a week-long, nonstop celebration in which locals dress up in traditional costume, the women in vibrantly coloured gypsy dresses. During the day, you can watch them parade around the fairground in carriages or on horseback, each coquettishly frilled and beribboned number more of a show stopper than the last. Bullfights are held in the bullring, with big-name matadors performing in some of the best line-ups of the season. In the evenings, and for most of the night, thousands throng the *casetas* – pavilions set up along the banks of the Río Guadalquivir – to eat, drink sherry and dance *sevillanas*, a home-grown variation of flamenco.

25.0796, 121.542456
**TAIPEI,
TAIWAN**

Built as a shrine to commemorate the man that – admire him or loathe him – did more to create modern Taiwan than any other, the Chiang Kai-Shek Memorial Hall sits at the centre of a grand monumental plaza in downtown Taipei. The hall contains a giant bronze statue of the Generalissimo under a lofty red cypress wood ceiling; though it seems a bit like a mausoleum, Chiang isn't buried inside, but his image is guarded by scary-looking troops nonetheless. The meticulously choreographed changing of the guard ceremony takes place every hour and has become something of a tourist spectacle, each soldier taking slow, ponderous steps in reverential silence. It's a tough job; not only do the soldiers have to stand motionless for hours and ignore the flashing cameras, their presence here is itself controversial. In 2007, the independence-leaning government renamed the site "National Taiwan Democracy Memorial Hall" and the guards were removed; after the KMT party regained power in 2008, the guards returned and the old name was restored.

40.740350, -73.994753
**NEW YORK CITY,
USA**

Don't be fooled by the name – the New York Halloween Parade isn't about ghosts and ghouls. Since it began in 1973, the annual October 31 mega-bash has evolved into an exuberant celebration of artistic expression – more like a carnival than a commemoration of all things eerie. Thousands descend on the city from all over the world to join in the fun and, most of all, to dress up – this has to be the largest and most elaborate costume party on the planet. Some opt for tradition – demons and ghosts, wizards and witches – but just about anything goes, from the historic (Roman soldiers, World War II uniforms and pirates) to the exotic (geishas and Rio-inspired plumed headdresses); from Hollywood (Disney characters, Star Wars favourites and superheroes) to the surreal, with enterprising partygoers recruiting their friends to come as packs of cards, furry animals or scrabble tiles.

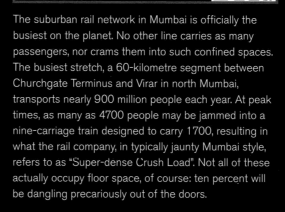

Transport

When two trains empty on the same platform at the same time at Churchgate Station you get a dense river of commuters flowing towards the exit, yet no one ever seems to rush or trip up. I wanted to get a shot showing the stream of colour that issues from the so-called "Ladies Carriage", where female commuters travel to avoid gropers. It took a week to obtain the necessary permission, and another three days to nail this rush-hour shot.

Dave Abram, *Photographer for The Rough Guide to South India*

18.934075, 72.827607
**MUMBAI,
INDIA**

The suburban rail network in Mumbai is officially the busiest on the planet. No other line carries as many passengers, nor crams them into such confined spaces. The busiest stretch, a 60-kilometre segment between Churchgate Terminus and Virar in north Mumbai, transports nearly 900 million people each year. At peak times, as many as 4700 people may be jammed into a nine-carriage train designed to carry 1700, resulting in what the rail company, in typically jaunty Mumbai style, refers to as "Super-dense Crush Load". Not all of these actually occupy floor space, of course: ten percent will be dangling precariously out of the doors.

40.757364, -73.985871
**NEW YORK CITY,
USA**

New Yorkers have a love-hate relationship with the city's taxis, a fast, fierce, yellow fleet of over 13,000. When you need them, taxis are always there (except, curiously, when it rains). On the other hand, when you don't need them, taxis are always there. Most of Midtown's gridlock is from cabs – a honking, belching sea of yellow – and their speeds can make crossing a New York City street a perilous activity. (It surprised no one when a former New York City cab driver went on to win the Indy 500 race.) But, there's good reason the word "iconic" is so often used to describe the cabs. Second perhaps only to money, taxis are what make the city run. Compared to spiking rents and $18 cocktails, taxis are still one of the better deals in Manhattan, and also something of an equalizer: the seats have been warmed by everyone from high-society "ladies who lunch" to East Village musicians hauling home their instruments. But even these ultimate urban machines are changing with the times. The city has ambitious plans to replace the traditional "Crown Victorias" with hybrid cars. The cabs may go green, but they'll always be yellow.

16.575736, 104.755819
**SAVANNAKHET,
LAOS**

Though Laos has been communist since the revolution of 1975, Buddhism continues to play a central role. Over sixty percent of the population are practising Theravada Buddhists and saffron-robed monks and novices are a common sight. In fact most Lao males get ordained at some point in their lives – usually for three months, and typically before they get married – which not only gives them status in the community but, more importantly, accrues karmic merit both for themselves and the women in their family. They must uphold the Buddhist precepts, refraining from sex, alcohol and other obvious indulgences, and spend part of every day in meditation; in politically hardline Laos, monks must also study Marxist-Leninist theory alongside the ancient Buddhist texts. Many young boys are sent to the monasteries to get a decent education, and the school at Savannakhet's biggest temple, Wat Sainyaphum, has a particularly good reputation. Though you wouldn't know it from the quiet, traffic-free streets, Savannakhet is Laos' third biggest city, and an important junction for trade and travel between Thailand and Vietnam. The Thai town of Mukdahan is a brief motorbike ride away, just a few minutes' west across the Mekong River, while to the east, Route 9 makes a beeline for Vietnam, 240km beyond.

35.691338, 139.700378
SHINJUKU STATION,
TOKYO, JAPAN

When you're pushed for time in Tokyo, the whole notion of space goes out of the window. One minute you're checking into a capsule hotel, the next you're folding yourself through the doors of a packed subway train, certain there's room for one more. But down beneath the world's busiest train station, inside one of the brilliant white carriages, it's survival of the fittest. Your toes will get stepped on. Your face will be squeezed against the window. And, if you don't find a suitable handrail, you'll find yourself being held upright by the sheer number of passengers. But conquer your claustrophobia and you'll learn a lot on the rush-hour subway. It's a place for spotting trends – the tamagotchi and Pokémon emerged from these tunnels – and exploring the Japanese psyche. You'll realize how calm the commuters are, despite all the chaos around them, and actually start enjoying the ride.

14.558256, -90.740258
CAMIONETAS,
GUATEMALA

With no passenger trains and few people able to afford a car, virtually everyone travels by "chicken bus" in Guatemala. Easily distinguished by their trademark clouds of thick, black, noxious fumes and rasping exhausts, these buses, also known as known as *camionetas*, are all old North American school buses, built to ferry under-eights from casa to classroom. Once they move down to these parts, they're decked out with gaudy "go-faster" stripes and windshield stickers bearing religious mantras ("Jesús es el Señor"). Comfort, however, is not customizable: there's limited legroom, and the seats and aisles are usually crammed with passengers (on the chicken bus, there's no such thing as "maximum capacity"). The driver always seems to be a moustachioed ladino with an eye for the ladies and a fixation for speed and overtaking on blind corners, while his helper (*ayundante*) is generally overworked and underage. It's the *ayundante*'s job to scramble up to the roof to retrieve your rucksack, collect the fares, and bellow out the destination. While travel by chicken bus may be uncomfortable, it's never dull, with chickens clucking, music assaulting your eardrums, and street vendors streaming down the aisles, offering everything from *chuchitos* (mini tamales) to bibles.

-6.159890, 39.186087
STONE TOWN, ZANZIBAR, TANZANIA

Cradled by the monsoon winds, East Africa has been trading with the outside world for at least five millennia, though it was the Persians who introduced the lateen-rigged vessel that became the maritime emblem of East Africa: the dhow. Ancient methods of construction, which survived until the 1930s, dictated that iron nails could not be used, supposedly for fear of the supposed magnetic effects of the ocean floor. Instead of nails, vessels were sewn or lashed together using coconut fibre, the gaps being filled with pounded fibre, mangrove bark and lime. The slanted triangular sails were made of woven palm leaves. At up to 15m in length, long-prowed *jahazi* dhows were the largest and grandest of East Africa's sailing ships; launches were accompanied by animal sacrifices and much celebration. Few *jahazis* are built today, but one or two examples can still be seen afloat. Apart from iron nails, modern methods and tools remain unchanged from those used two thousand years ago.

14.359152, 98.920341

**DEATH RAILWAY,
THAILAND**

Shortly after entering World War II in December 1941, Japan began looking for a supply route to connect its newly acquired territories, stretching from Singapore to the Burma–India border. Despite the almost impenetrable terrain, the River Kwai basin was chosen as the route for a new Thailand–Burma Railway, and about 60,000 Allied POWs were shipped in to work on the link, their numbers later augmented by as many as 200,000 Asian labourers. Some three million cubic metres of rock were shifted and 14km of bridges built with little else but picks and shovels, dynamite and pulleys. By the time the line was completed, fifteen months later in October 1943, it had more than earned its nickname, the Death Railway: an estimated 16,000 POWs and 100,000 Asian labourers died of overwork, starvation or disease while working on it – one man, it is said, for every sleeper laid on the track. As if to underscore its tragic futility, the railway saw less than two years of active service: after the Japanese surrender on August 15, 1945, it came under the jurisdiction of the British who, thinking it would be used to supply Karen separatists in Burma, tore up 4km of track, thereby cutting the rail link forever.

10.921034, 107.868919

THE REUNIFICATION EXPRESS, VIETNAM

It takes at least 29 hours for the Reunification Express to chug its way down the length of Vietnam, from Hanoi in the north to the southern hub of Ho Chi Minh City, so there's plenty of time to get to know your fellow passengers. At least eight trains a day make the 1726-kilometre journey; time it right from the capital, Hanoi, and you'll board in the evening, ready to bed down on your bunk – one of six if you're braving the (door-less) hard-sleeper class, or a spacious foursome in a soft sleeper, with optional air-con. Having crossed the notorious 17th parallel near Dong Ha – until 1975 the demarcation line between communist North Vietnam and the American-backed South – you'll wake to the best of the scenery. Skirting the coastline between the elegant imperial capital, Hue, and the port city of Da Nang, the train labours up and over Hai Van Pass, with views encompassing rugged shorelines and misty hilltops, before regaining the familiar lowland pattern of palms and paddies. Dawn on the second day finally brings into sight the chaos of Ho Chi Minh City – or Saigon, as timetables and locals still call it. Forty years ago the city was at bitter war with Hanoi, now the two are peacefully linked once again, by the Reunification Express.

13.360854, 103.861828

SIEM REAP, CAMBODIA

Clapped-out minibuses are a popular – and cheap – mode of transport in Cambodia, departing only when absolutely packed, with people, goods and livestock piled inside, on the roof and hanging out of the back. Fares are lower still if you're prepared to rough it on the back of a pick-up truck. These workhorses of the Cambodian transport system convey people and goods over the bumpiest of roads and tracks, even along riverbeds or up rocky hillsides. Passengers sit on (or fit around) the goods being transported, and are bounced around with nothing much to grab hold of. Plenty of water and a sense of humour are essential; those in the know also wrap a scarf round the face to keep out the dust.

25.267236, 55.302912

DUBAI,
UNITED ARAB EMIRATES

Despite contemporary Dubai's obsession with the marvels of modern technology, getting from one side of the Creek to the other in the city centre is still a charmingly old-fashioned experience, involving a trip across the waters in one of the hundreds of rickety little boats – or *abras* – which ferry passengers between Deira and Bur Dubai. It's a wonderful journey, offering superb views of the fascinating muddle of Creekside buildings with their tangles of souks, wind towers, mosques and minarets – and is certainly the most fun you can have in Dubai for 50 fils. Bumps and minor collisions between boats are common when docking and departing, so take care, or you might find yourself not so much up the Creek as in it.

34.558274, -115.743751

CALIFORNIA,
USA

Eighty years since it was first completed, seventy since John Steinbeck called it "the mother road, the road of flight" in *The Grapes of Wrath*, and sixty since songwriter Bobby Troup set it all down in rhyme, what better reason to visit Southwest USA could there be than to get hip to this timely tip, and get your kicks on Route 66? The heyday of Route 66 as the nation's premier cross-country route – winding from Chicago to LA – lasted barely twenty years, from its being paved in 1937 until it began to be superseded by freeways in 1957. It was officially rendered defunct in 1984, when Williams, Arizona, became the last town to be bypassed. Nonetheless, substantial stretches of the original Route 66 survive, complete with the motels and drive-ins that became icons of vernacular American architecture. Restored 1950s roadsters and the latest Harley-Davidsons alike flock to cruise along the atmospheric, neon-lit frontages of towns such as Albuquerque and Flagstaff, or through such empty desertscapes as those between Grants and Gallup in New Mexico, or Seligman and Kingman in Arizona.

39.941428, 116.386113
BEIJING,
CHINA

Getting around Beijing can be a challenge. The public transport system is extensive but overstretched and the streets are nearing gridlock – the average speed of a car is less than 10mph. By far the best way to get around is to hire a bike, and nowhere more so than in the area north of the centre of Beijing – the only district where the city's traditional street plan, a tangle of *hutongs*, has been preserved on any scale. Traffic within the *hutongs* is light, and you're free to dive into any alley you fancy. You're almost certain to get lost, but in doing so you'll discover Beijing's other, more private, face: among the cluttered, grey alleyways are poky courtyards, converted palaces and small open spaces where old men sit with caged pet birds.

38.301868, -122.283894
NAPA VALLEY,
CALIFORNIA

Trains first chugged along the tracks of the Napa Valley in the 1860s to bring guests to the hot springs resort of Calistoga, before the wineries usurped the town as the region's star turn. The influence that rail transport has had over Napa's development is plain to see from the picture windows of the Napa Valley Wine Train: acres of vineyards and wineries are testimony to the region's reliance on the grape. American wine sales are worth over $21 billion, and California produces nearly two out of every three bottles produced. The 60-kilometre round trip is a great way for both wine novices and seasoned oenophiles to get the lie of the land before a spot of winery-hopping in the Valley, and there's no shortage of tasting opportunities on board too. A list of some thirty wines is available to whet your appetite, and "wine educators" are on hand if you don't know your Pinot Noir from your Zinfandel.

45.433161, 12.324364
**VENICE,
ITALY**

Venice is notoriously one of the world's most expensive cities to visit – but it's also one of the priciest to live in. Any stuff on sale in a Venetian shop is likely to have arrived there in three stages: by lorry to the docks; then by boat to the canalside nearest to the shop; and then by hand-barrow to the doorway, a procedure that often involves hauling the load over several bridges. Every leg of the journey, of course, adds a mark-up to the price the customer pays. At least with the San Barnaba grocery barge, the supply chain is a less arduous transfer from lorry to boat to a second boat. The Rialto bridge is a good vantage point from which to watch the to-ing and fro-ing of all manner of cargo – particularly in the morning, when barges and motorboats ferry fruit, veg and fish to the city's main market, weaving around the vaporetti (water-buses) to get to the quaysides.

44.173386, 5.276613

**MONT VENTOUX,
FRANCE**

From the Rhône and Durance valleys, the outline of Mont
Ventoux is an unmissable beacon on the horizon. White
with snow, black with storm-cloud shadow or reflecting
myriad shades of blue, the barren pebbles of the uppermost
300m are like a weather vane for all of western Provence.
Winds can accelerate to 250km per hour around the
meteorological, TV and military masts and dishes on the
summit, but if you can stand still for a moment the view in
all directions is unbelievable. Not surprisingly, the winds are
even more of a problem for those on two wheels: its fame as
a scene of one of the most gruelling climbs of the Tour de
France has made it notorious among cyclists.

9.461905, 76.394634

KUTTANAD, KERALA

An immense labyrinth of interconnecting canals, islets, paddy fields, glassy lagoons and inland lakes, the Kuttanad backwaters of central and southern Kerala encompass a landscape and way of life unique in India. Nowhere else will you encounter Orthodox Syrian-Christian bishops with Father Christmas beards rushing to mass in speedboats, huge flocks of domestic ducks being shepherded by their owners from canoes, coir-makers punting rafts of coconut husks to market or crews of 150 bare-chested men racing medieval longboats against a backdrop of dense palm forest. Whether you travel around in local diesel-powered ferries, converted rice barges or canoes, scenes of everyday domestic life on riverbanks are what linger longest in the memory: kids being paddled to school, their satchels piled high on the bows of slender dugouts; women soaping down babies or thumping piles of washing on the front steps of little red-tiled houses; fishermen diving for clams; and itinerant vegetable vendors haggling with travellers on the river.

50.090889, 14.409480

PRAGUE, CZECH REPUBLIC

Prague's metro is one of the few positive legacies of the communist era. Soviet-designed, it's spacious, fast, futuristic – in a 1970s Star Trek kind of way – and run with an efficiency that even the Swiss would be proud of. What's more, it's also one of the busiest metros in Europe, with over 1.5 million passengers a day – more than the population of the city itself. Its safety announcement, while not quite as pithy as London's "Mind the Gap", is embedded in every Czech's memory bank: "Ukončete, prosím, výstup a nástup, dveře se zavírají" ("Finish, please, getting on and off, the doors are closing"). Shortly after the collapse of the communist system in 1989, 14 stations had their names changed to more ideologically neutral ones, and nowadays very little remains to remind the casual commuter of the communist period; even the old Soviet rolling stock has either been refurbished by Skoda or replaced by Siemens.

Credits

Activities

Hawkes passage, Malolo Barrier Reef p.6. *Photo:* Chris Christoforou *Text:* Ian Osborn

Dune buggy, Huachina dunes p.8. *Photo:* Tim Draper *Text:* Dilwyn Jenkins

Rollercoaster, Parque de Atracciones, Madrid p.9. *Photo:* Tim Draper *Text:* Brendon Griffin

Football, Boca p.10. *Photo:* Greg Roden *Text:* Andrew Benson & Rosalba O'Brien

Walk from Col de la Croix to Girolata p.11. *Photo & Text:* David Abram

Hang-gliding, Rio de Janeiro p.12. *Photo:* Roger d'Olivere Mapp *Text:* Joe Tyrrell

Bungee-jumping, Llano del Rosario p.13. *Photo:* Greg Roden *Text:* Keith Drew

Cycling, Florence p.14. *Photo:* Roger d'Olivere Mapp *Text:* Helena Smith

Rollerskating, London p.15. *Photo:* Roger d'Olivere Mapp *Text:* James Smart

White-water rafting, Kaituna River p.16. *Photo:* Paul Whitfield *Text:* Tony Mudd & Paul Whitfield

Kataw, Savannakhet p.17. *Photo:* Tim Draper *Text:* Steven Vickers

Rock-climbing, Joshua Tree National Park p.18. *Photo & Text:* Paul Whitfield

Horse-riding, Wadi Rum p.19. *Photo:* Jean-Christophe Godet *Text:* Matthew Teller

Bronte swimming baths, Sydney p.20. *Photo:* Helena Smith *Text:* Paul Whitfield

Copacabana beach life p.21. *Photo:* Roger d'Olivere Mapp *Text:* Rob Coates & Oliver Marshall

Nad Al Sheba Racecourse, Dubai p.22. *Photo & Text:* Gavin Thomas

Zorbing, Agrodome Adventure Park, Rotorua p.23. *Photo:* Paul Whitfield *Text:* Tony Mudd & Paul Whitfield

Naknek Lake, Alaska p.24. *Photo & Text:* Paul Whitfield

Gower Peninsula, Wales p.25. *Photo:* Scott Stickland *Text:* Mike Parker

Kalarippayattu, Kerala p.26. *Photo:* Tim Draper *Text:* David Abram

Hot-air ballooning, Rocamadour p.27. *Photo:* Jean-Christophe Godet *Text:* Richard Hammond

Belief

Blue Mosque, Istanbul p.28. *Photo:* Roger d'Olivere Mapp *Text:* Terry Richardson

Punta Arenas cemetery p.30. *Photo:* Tim Draper *Text:* Melissa Graham

Salvation Mountain, California p.31. *Photo & Text:* Paul Whitfield

Deir al-Suryani monastery, Wadi Natrun p.32. *Photo:* Eddie Gerald *Text:* Dan Richardson

Monk, Savannakhet p.33. *Photo:* Tim Draper *Text:* Jeff Cranmer

Church of the Saviour on Spilled Blood, St Petersburg p.34. *Photo:* Jonathan Smith *Text:* Rob Humphreys

The Wishes fireworks show at Disney's Magic Kingdom p.35. *Photo:* Dan Bannister *Text:* Ross Velton

The Jockey Club, Rio de Janeiro p.36. *Photo:* Roger d'Olivere Mapp *Text:* Rob Coates

Convento dei Cappuccini catacombs, Palermo p.37. *Photo:* Jon Cunningham *Text:* Jules Brown

Worshippers at Cao Dai cathedral, Tay Ninh p.38. *Photo:* Tim Draper *Text:* Mark Lewis

Rameshwaram temple colonnade, Tamil Nadu p.39. *Photo:* Tim Draper *Text:* Nick Edwards

Buddha, Golden Temple, Dambulla p.40. *Photo & Text:* Gavin Thomas

Supporters at the Maracanã Stadium, Rio de Janeiro p.41. *Photo:* Roger d'Olivere Mapp *Text:* Rob Coates & Oliver Marshall

Theyyam ritual dance near Kunnur, Kerala p.42. *Photo:* Tim Draper *Text:* David Abram

Hassidic Jew at the Wailing Wall, Jerusalem p.43. *Photo:* Eddie Gerald *Text:* Roger Norum

Pilgrims visiting Esquipulas basilica p.44. *Photo:* Tim Draper *Text:* Iain Stewart

Mosquée Hassan II, Casablanca p.45. *Photo:* Suzanne Porter *Text:* Mark Ellingham

King Hussein Mosque, Amman p.46. *Photo:* Jean-Christophe Godet *Text:* Matthew Teller

Shoes at the Woljeongsa Temple, Odaesan National Park, South Korea p.47. *Photo:* Tim Draper *Text:* Martin Zatko

Prayer flags, Waterloo Temple p.48. *Photo:* Sean Edghill *Text:* Polly Thomas

Sadhu, Kathmandu p.49. *Photo:* Tim Draper *Text:* Shafik Meghji

Everyday life

Fisherman casting net, Don Det, Laos p.50. *Photo:* Tim Draper *Text:* Lucy Ridout

Leith waterside p.52. *Photo:* Helena Smith *Text:* Donald Reid

Food stall, Naples historic centre p.53. *Photo:* Karen Trist *Text:* Natasha Foges

Selfridges food hall p.54. *Photo:* Suzanne Porter *Text:* Rob Humphreys

Street performers, Havana, Cuba p.55. *Photo:* Lydia Evans *Text:* Brendon Griffin

View of San Frediano, Florence p.56. *Photo:* Roger d'Olivere Mapp *Text:* Jonathan Buckley

Tanneries, Fes p.57. *Photo:* Suzanne Porter *Text:* Mark Ellingham

Man with camel, Rajasthan p.58. *Photo:* Simon Bracken *Text:* Gavin Thomas

Hair salon, Double Bay, Sydney p.59. *Photo:* Guy Bailey *Text:* Paul Whitfield

Madrid by night p.60. *Photo:* Tim Draper *Text:* Mark Ellingham

Women farming seaweed, Bwejuu, East Unguja, Zanzibar p.61. *Photo:* Suzanne Porter *Text:* Jens Finke

Ciego de Avila, Cuba p.62. *Photo:* Lydia Evans *Text:* Fiona McAuslan & Matthew Norman

Street scene, Daegu, South Korea p.63. *Photo:* Tim Draper *Text:* Martin Zatko

Rio de Janeiro p.64. *Photo:* Roger d'Olivere Mapp *Text:* Rob Coates & Oliver Marshall

Snail stew stall, Jemaa el Fna, Marrakesh p.65. *Photo:* Suzanne Porter *Text:* Mark Ellingham

Soldiers on Matzu-bound ferry p.66. *Photo:* Brice Minnigh *Text:* Stephen Keeling

Balik Pazarı, Istanbul p.67. *Photo:* Roger d'Olivere Mapp *Text:* Terry Richardson

Tokyo commuters p.68. *Photo:* Martin Richardson *Text:* Steven Vickers

Plantation, Kerala p.69. *Photo:* Tim Draper *Text:* Dave Abram

Food & drink

Dry Martini bar, Barcelona p.70. *Photo:* Chris Christoforou *Text:* Jules Brown

Chichicastenango market p.72. *Photo:* Tim Draper *Text:* Iain Stewart

Fishermen, Skala du Port, Essaouira p.73. *Photo:* Suzanne Porter *Text:* Mark Ellingham & Daniel Jacobs

Luk Yu Teahouse, Hong Kong p.74. *Photo:* Karen Trist *Text:* David Leffman

Sucre restaurant, Belgrano, Buenos Aires p.75. *Photo:* Greg Roden *Text:* Andrew Benson & Rosalba O'Brien

Tea at the Ritz p.76. *Photo:* Suzanne Porter *Text:* Rob Humphreys

Making opium tea in a Bishnoi village outside Jodhpur, Rajasthan p.77. *Photo:* Simon Bracken *Text:* Daniel Jacobs & Gavin Thomas

Kioscos, eastern Puerto Rico p.78. *Photo:* Tim Draper *Text:* Stephen Keeling

Lombardi's, New York p.79. *Photo:* Angus Oborn *Text:* Richard Koss

Ice-cream sign, Rome p.80. *Photo:* Natascha Sturny *Text:* Natasha Foges

Oktoberfest, Munich p.81. *Photo:* Demetrio Carrasco *Text:* Neville Walker

Welling Café, Amsterdam p.82. *Photo:* Mark Thomas *Text:* Martin Dunford

Hue market, Vietnam p.83. *Photo:* Tim Draper *Text:* Jan Dodd

Riverside food stalls, Vientiane, Laos p.84. *Photo:* Tim Draper *Text:* Jeff Cranmer

La Gare restaurant, Paris p.85. *Photo:* James McConnachie *Text:* Ruth Blackmore

Tea, Beijing p.86. *Photo:* Tim Draper *Text:* Simon Lewis

Katz's Deli, New York p.87. *Photo:* Susannah Sayler *Text:* Natasha Foges

Skybar, Bangkok p.88. *Photo:* Karen Trist *Text:* Paul Gray

Saray patisserie, Istanbul p.89. *Photo:* Roger d'Olivere Mapp *Text:* Terry Richardson

Keepsakes

Tribal market, Louang Phabang, Laos p.90. *Photo:* Tim Draper *Text:* Steven Vickers

Varadero, Cuba p.92. *Photo:* Lydia Evans *Text:* Fiona McAuslan & Matthew Norman

St-Ouen market, Paris p.93. *Photo:* Lydia Evans *Text:* James McConnachie

Bread in anime character can, Akihabara, Tokyo p.94. *Photo:* Martin Richardson *Text:* Steven Vickers

Store Bay craft stalls, Tobago p.95. *Photo:* Sean Edghill *Text:* Polly Thomas

Carpets, Holiday Centre mall, Dubai p.96. *Photo & Text:* Gavin Thomas

Buddha souvenir, Banglamphu, Bangkok p.97. *Photo:* Karen Trist *Text:* Lucy Ridout

Fighting cock statues at base of statue of King Naresuan, Ayutthaya p.98. *Photo:* Karen Trist *Text:* Lucy Ridout

Flamenco aprons, Seville p.99. *Photo:* Georgie Scott *Text:* Jan Fairley, David Locos & Manuel Dominguez

Dragon souvenir, Chinatown, San Francisco p.100. *Photo:* Greg Roden *Text:* Mark Ellwood

Clay Figures, tourist market, Havana Vieja p.101. *Photo:* Lydia Evans *Text:* Fiona McAuslan & Matthew Norman

Nautical antiques store, Portland, Maine p.102. *Photo:* Dan Bannister *Text:* Stephen Keeling

Products for sale at Pisac Market, near Cusco p.103. *Photo:* Tim Draper *Text:* Dilwyn Jenkins

Moroccan silverware, Marrakesh p.104. *Photo:* Suzanne Porter *Text:* Mark Ellingham

Beaded dresses for sale, Chiang Mai night market p.105. *Photo:* Karen Trist *Text:* Paul Gray

Panjiayuan antiques market, southeast Beijing p.106. *Photo:* Tim Draper *Text:* Simon Lewis

Venetian mask p.107. *Photo:* Martin Richardson *Text:* Jonathan Buckley

Nature

Jaguar, Guatemala p.108. *Photo:* Tim Draper *Text:* Iain Stewart

Moeraki Boulders, Otago p.110. *Photo:* Paul Whitfield *Text:* Tony Mudd & Paul Whitfield

Mountain stream in the Retezat Mountains, Transylvania p.111. *Photo:* Gregory Wrona *Text:* Norm Longley & Tim Burford

Tufa towers, Mono Lake p.112. *Photo & Text:* Paul Whitfield

Field of sunflowers near Eymet, Dordogne p.113. *Photo:* Jean-Christophe Godet *Text:* Richard Hammond

Cat Bells, Derwent Water p.114. *Photo & Text:* Helena Smith

Falcon, Château Les Milandes, the Dordogne p.115. *Photo:* Jean-Christophe Godet *Text:* Jan Dodd

Pink rock, Petra p.116. *Photo:* Jean-Christophe Godet *Text:* Matthew Teller

Roccapina beach, Corsica p.117. *Photo & Text:* David Abram

Cholla cactus, Joshua Tree National Park p.118. *Photo & Text:* Paul Whitfield

Beachy Head p.119. *Photo:* Tim Draper *Text:* Robert Andrews

Shipwreck Bay, Zakynthos p.120. *Photo:* Michelle Grant *Text:* Nick Edwards & John Gill

Volcano Irazú National Park, Costa Rica p.121. *Photo:* Greg Roden *Text:* Jean McNeil

Waterlilies, Sukhothai Historical Park p.122. *Photo:* Karen Trist *Text:* Lucy Ridout

Interior of Candelaria caves, Guatemala p.123. *Photo:* Tim Draper *Text:* Iain Stewart

Buddha in bodhi tree, Ayutthaya p.124. *Photo:* Karen Trist *Text:* Paul Gray

Active lava flow, Kilauea volcano, Hawaii p.125. *Photo & Text:* Greg Ward

Interior of Gruta de las Maravillas, Aracena p.126. *Photo:* Georgie Scott *Text:* Geoff Garvey

Salar de Surie, Chile p.127. *Photo:* Tim Draper *Text:* Melissa Graham

Welchman Hall Gully, Barbados p.128. *Photo:* Ian Cummings *Text:* Adam Vaitlingam

Cathedral Rock, Dinosaur National Monument, Colorado p.129. *Photo & Text:* Christian Williams

IJsselmeer near Medemblik, The Netherlands p.130. *Photo:* Tim Draper *Text:* Martin Dunford

The Sisteron Gap, Provence p.131. *Photo:* Michelle Grant *Text:* Neville Walker

Kelso Dunes, Mojave National Preserve, California p.132. *Photo & Text:* Paul Whitfield

Franz Josef Glacier, West Coast New Zealand p.133. *Photo:* Paul Whitfield *Text:* Tony Mudd & Paul Whitfield

People

Matmata pit-dweller, Tunisia p.134. *Photo:* Roger d'Olivere Mapp *Text:* Tristan Rutherford

Jimmy Woo's, Amsterdam p.136. *Photo:* Mark Thomas *Text:* Roísín Cameron

Fiesta de la Virgen de Carmen, Paucartambo, Peru p.137. *Photo:* Tim Draper *Text:* Dilwyn Jenkins

Boy on Copacabana beach p.138. *Photo:* Roger d'Olivere Mapp *Text:* Rob Coates & Oliver Marshall

Tippu Tipp's House, Stone Town, Zanzibar p.139. *Photo:* Suzanne Porter *Text:* Jens Finke

St Lucian woman p.140. *Photo:* Roger d'Olivere Mapp *Text:* Natalie Folster

Wild crowd at La Tomatina, Buñol p.141. *Photo:* Demetrio Carrasco *Text:*
AnneLise Sorensen
Gauchos, Buenos Aires p.142. *Photo:* Greg Roden *Text:* Andrew Benson &
Rosalba O'Brien
Opera singer at the Liyuan Theatre, Beijing p.143. *Photo:* Tim Draper *Text:*
Simon Lewis
Lady in red, Lucca p.144. *Photo:* Roger d'Olivere Mapp *Text:* Helena Smith
Club Parade, Ibiza Town, Ibiza p.145. *Photo:* Lydia Evans *Text:* Iain Stewart
Ixil woman from Nebaj, Guatemala p.146. *Photo:* Tim Draper *Text:* Iain Stewart
Snake charmer by waterfall, Setti Fatma, Morocco p.147. *Photo:* Suzanne Porter
Text: James Stewart
Bhaktapur, near Kathmandu, Nepal p.148. *Photo:* Tim Draper *Text:* James McConnachie
José Garrido García, Museo del Mar Caracoles, Sanlucar de Barrameda p.149.
Photo: Georgie Scott *Text:* Geoff Garvey
Gurung tribeswoman, Ghandruk village, Nepal p.150. *Photo:* Tim Draper *Text:*
James McConnachie
Children at a plantation, Kerala, South India p.151. *Photo:* Tim Draper *Text:*
Gavin Thomas

Structures
Dome of San Luis de los Franceses, Seville p.152. *Photo:* Georgie Scott *Text:*
Keith Drew
Swimmer at the Pont du Gard p.154. *Photo:* Jean-Christophe Godet *Text:*
Neville Walker
Edificio Barolo on Avenida de Mayo, Monserrat, Buenos Aires p.155. *Photo:* Greg
Roden *Text:* Andrew Benson & Rosalba O'Brien
Model Prison, Isla de la Juventud, Cuba p.156. *Photo:* Lydia Evans *Text:* Fiona
McAuslan & Matthew Norman
Chihuly chandelier, the Bellagio hotel, Las Vegas p.157. *Photo & Text:* Greg Ward
Floralis Generica in Recoleta, Buenos Aires p.158. *Photo:* Greg Roden *Text:*
Andrew Benson & Rosalba O'Brien
Basilica Cistern, Istanbul p.159. *Photo:* Roger d'Olivere Mapp *Text:* Terry Richardson
Grand Hyatt hotel, Jinmao Tower, Shanghai p.160. *Photo:* Tim Draper *Text:*
Simon Lewis
Inca Terracing at Moray, in the Sacred Valley near Cusco p.161. *Photo:* Tim Draper
Text: Dilwyn Jenkins
Ruvanvalisaya dagoba, Anuradhapura p.162. *Photo & Text:* Gavin Thomas
Stata Center at MIT, Cambridge, Massachusetts p.163. *Photo:* Angus Oborn *Text:*
Sarah Hull
Monastery facade, Petra p.164. *Photo:* Jean-Christophe Godet *Text:*
Matthew Teller
Rollercoaster, Knott's Berry Farm, Los Angeles p.165. *Photo:* Demetrio Carrasco
Text: Jeff Dickey
Niemeyer museum, Niteroi p.166. *Photo:* Roger d'Olivere Mapp *Text:* Rob Coates
& Oliver Marshall
Eiffel Tower by night, Paris p.167. *Photo:* Lydia Evans *Text:* James McConnachie
Aqualand waterpark, Magaluf, Mallorca p.168. *Photo:* Simon Bracken *Text:* Phil Lee

Uros Islands, southern Peru p.169. *Photo:* Tim Draper *Text:* Dilwyn Jenkins
Due Torri, view from San Donato hotel, Bologna p.170. *Photo:* Martin Richardson
Text: Natasha Foges
Hallgrímskirkja, Reykjavík p.171. *Photo:* David Leffman *Text:* James Proctor
View of Chicago by night from the Signature Room bar p.172. *Photo:* Greg Roden
Text: Shea Dean
Canalside buildings, Ghent p.173. *Photo:* Jean-Christophe Godet *Text:* Phil Lee
Palafitos, Castro p.174. *Photo:* Tim Draper *Text:* Melissa Graham
Monument aux Girondins, Bordeaux p.175. *Photo:* Jean-Christophe Godet *Text:*
Jan Dodd

Time-wasting
TV Corner, Stone Town p.176. *Photo:* Suzanne Porter *Text:* Jens Finke
Tivoli, Copenhagen p.178. *Photo:* Helena Smith *Text:* Caroline Osborne
Roxie diner, Buenos Aires p.179. *Photo:* Greg Roden *Text:* Rosalba O'Brien
Marina Piccola beach, Capri p.180. *Photo:* Karen Trist *Text:* Martin Dunford
Kouang Si falls, Louang Phabang p.181. *Photo:* Tim Draper *Text:* Jeff Cranmer
Ice cream seller, Benaulim beach p.182. *Photo & Text:* David Abram
Bournemouth beach p.183. *Photo:* Tim Draper *Text:* Rob Andrews
Boys diving in the Bosphorus p.184. *Photo:* Roger d'Olivere Mapp *Text:*
Kathryn Tomasetti
Pier, Daytona Beach, Florida p.185. *Photo:* Demetrio Carrasco *Text:* Ross Velton
Pelican Bar, Treasure Brach p.186. *Photo & Text:* Polly Thomas
Coffee bar, Columbus Avenue, San Francisco p.187. *Photo:* Angus Oborn *Text:*
Mark Ellwood
Chowpatty Beach, Mumbai p.188. *Photo & Text:* David Abram
Thermal pool in Bâile Felix p.189. *Photo:* Gregory Wrona *Text:* Norm Longley &
Tim Burford
Men on a bench, Jerez p.190. *Photo:* Georgie Scott *Text:* Keith Drew
El Paraíso beach club, Tulum p.191. *Photo:* Sarah Cummins *Text:* Roger Norum
Cyclos in Phnom Penh p.192. *Photo:* Tim Draper *Text:* Lucy Ridout
Playing dominoes in Soufriere p.193. *Photo:* Roger d'Olivere Mapp *Text:*
Skye Hernandez

Tourist trail
The Mona Lisa in the frame p.194. *Photo:* Lydia Evans *Text:* James McConnachie
Aerial shot of the Setai hotel, Miami p.196. *Photo:* Anthony Pidgeon *Text:*
Mark Ellwood
Amber Fort, Rajasthan p.197. *Photo:* Simon Bracken *Text:* Gavin Thomas
Tourists at Senso-ji, Asakusa, Tokyo p.198. *Photo:* Martin Richardson *Text:*
Steven Vickers
Maspalomas dunes, Gran Canaria p.199. *Photo & Text:* Neville Walker
Lincoln Memorial, Washington DC p.200. *Photo:* Angus Oborn *Text:* Jules Brown
& Jeff Dickey
Outer Bay tank, Monterey Aquarium p.201. *Photo & Text:* Paul Whitfield
Walking in Wadi Rum p.202. *Photo:* Jean-Christophe Godet *Text:* Keith Drew
Hacienda Uayamon, Yucatán p.203. *Photo:* Dan Bannister *Text:* Roger Norum

Playa de Amadores, Gran Canaria p.204. *Photo & Text:* Neville Walker

Sunset ranger talk at Glacier Point, Yosemite National Park p.205. *Photo & Text:* Paul Whitfield

Reflection of Palazzo Vecchio & David, Piazza della Signoria, Florence p.206. *Photo:* Michelle Grant *Text:* Jonathan Buckley

Pilgrims bathing in the Tungabhadra, Hampi p.207. *Photo:* David Abram *Text:* Nick Edwards

Neon sign, Las Vegas p.208. *Photo:* Greg Roden *Text:* Greg Ward

The Himalaya, Annapurna Trek p.209. *Photo:* Tim Draper *Text:* Shafik Meghji

Casa di Fontana Piccola, Pompeii p.210. *Photo:* Karen Trist *Text:* Natasha Foges

Charging Bull statue, New York p.211. *Photo:* Curtis Hamilton *Text:* Richard Koss

Postcards, London p.212. *Photo:* Roger d'Olivere Mapp *Text:* James Smart

Korean Folk Village, traditional costume dance p.213. *Photo:* Tim Draper *Text:* Martin Zatko

View from the Empire State Building p.214. *Photo:* Susannah Sayler *Text:* Martin Dunford

Tourists climb Nohoch Mul, Yucatán p.215. *Photo:* Sarah Cummins *Text:* John Fisher

Buddha, Sop Ruak p.216. *Photo:* Karen Trist *Text:* Paul Gray

Staircase, Vatican Museums p.217. *Photo:* Natascha Sturny *Text:* Martin Dunford

Maid of the Mist, Niagara Falls p.218. *Photo:* Enrique Uranga *Text:* Nick Edwards

Hot-air balloon, the Serengeti p.219. *Photo:* Suzanne Porter *Text:* Jens Finke

Tradition

Windsor Rose tearoom, Mount Dora, Florida p.220. *Photo:* Dan Bannister *Text:* Ross Velton

Ixil children from Nebaj in traditional costume p.222. *Photo:* Tim Draper *Text:* Iain Stewart

Street parade at the Ponce festival p.223. *Photo:* Tim Draper *Text:* Stephen Keeling

Sumo wrestlers performing dohyo-iri (ring entering ceremony), Ryogoku, Tokyo p.224. *Photo:* Martin Richardson *Text:* Simon Richmond & Jan Dodd

Traditional wooden outrigger fishing boat, Benaulim beach p.225. *Photo & Text:* David Abram

Notting Hill Carnival, London p.226. *Photo:* Demetrio Carrasco *Text:* Polly Thomas

Close up of a bandoneón in San Telmo, Buenos Aires p.227. *Photo:* Greg Roden *Text:* Rosalba O'Brien

Kathakali performance, Kerala p.228. *Photo:* Tim Draper *Text:* David Abram

Flower Hmong at Bac Ha ethnic minority market, Vietnam p.229. *Photo:* Tim Draper *Text:* Martin Zatko & Michael Sieburg

San Sebastián Festival, San Juan p.230. *Photo:* Tim Draper *Text:* Stephen Keeling

Dragon kites around Tian'anmen Square, Beijing p.231. *Photo:* Tim Draper *Text:* Natasha Foges

Rodeo at San Fernando p.232. *Photo:* Tim Draper *Text:* Melissa Graham

Masked theatre at Hahoe folk village near Andong p.233. *Photo:* Tim Draper *Text:* Martin Zatko

Chinese opera performer paints his face to play the jing or warrior role p.234. *Photo:* Tim Draper *Text:* Simon Lewis

Las Fallas festival p.235. *Photo:* Damien Simonis *Text:* Dave Dakota & Damien Simonis

Carnaval, Rio de Janeiro p.236. *Photo:* Alex Robinson *Text:* Oliver Marshall

The Red Lion pub, London p.237. *Photo:* Roger d'Olivere Mapp *Text:* James Smart

Puppet, Museo della Marionette, Palermo p.238. *Photo:* Jon Cunningham *Text:* Robert Andrews

Flouncy dresses, Feria de Abril, Seville p.239. *Photo:* Damien Simonis *Text:* Geoff Garvey

Changing of the guard ceremony, Taipei p.240. *Photo:* Brice Minnigh *Text:* Stephen Keeling

Halloween Parade, New York p.241. *Photo:* Demetrio Carrasco *Text:* Stephen Keeling

Transport

Commuters, Churchgate Station, Mumbai p.242. *Photo & Text:* David Abram (Image copyright: David Abram)

Taxi cabs, Times Square, New York p.244. *Photo:* Curtis Hamilton *Text:* AnneLise Sorensen

Monk on bike, Savannakhet p.245. *Photo:* Tim Draper *Text:* Lucy Ridout

Rush hour on the JR line, Shinjuku station, Tokyo p.246. *Photo:* Martin Richardson *Text:* Steven Vickers

Chicken buses, Guatemala p.247. *Photo:* Tim Draper *Text:* Iain Stewart

Dhow, Stone Town p.248. *Photo:* Suzanne Porter *Text:* Jens Finke

Tourists walking along a trestle bridge section of the Death Railway p.249. *Photo:* Karen Trist *Text:* Lucy Ridout

Reunification Express, Vietnam p.250. *Photo:* Tim Draper *Text:* Lucy Ridout

Local people on a minibus, Siem Reap, Cambodia p.251. *Photo:* Tim Draper *Text:* Beverley Palmer

Al Sabkha abra station, Deira, Dubai p.252. *Photo & Text:* Gavin Thomas

Route 66, California p.253. *Photo:* Paul Whitfield *Text:* Greg Ward

Hutongs, Beijing p.254. *Photo:* Tim Draper *Text:* Simon Lewis

Napa Valley Wine Train, California p.255. *Photo:* Angus Oborn *Text:* Natasha Foges

San Barnaba grocery barge, Venice p.256. *Photo:* Martin Richardson *Text:* Jonathan Buckley

Mont Ventoux, Provence p.257. *Photo:* Michelle Grant *Text:* Neville Walker

Boats on the Backwaters, Kerala p.258. *Photo:* Tim Draper *Text:* David Abram

Malostranská metro, Prague p.259. *Photo:* Jon Cunningham *Text:* Rob Humphreys

axiom

photographic agency